SWINGING AND SLINGING

The Refugee and Business Success Stories of Jimmy's Egg CEO

Ban Nguyen

Swinging and Slinging: The Refugee and Business Success Stories of Jimmy's Egg CEO

Cover designed by Ava Wood, Fins and Feathers Designs
ISBN: 978-1-965142-49-3 (Paperback)
ISBN: 978-1-965142-50-9 (Hardback)
LCCN: 2025908119

Edmond, Oklahoma

To my wife, Yen, my oldest son, James, his wife Brandi, their son Mason, my middle son Khoi, his wife Julie, and my daughter Pauline.

Table of Contents

Introduction

Long before I ever cracked my first egg over a hot griddle, I was handed a tennis racket. It was love at first swing. My mother and father raised four boys among eight children, and all the boys played tennis. Some of my sisters, too, but the boys had no choice. As the youngest boy, I never even questioned it. All I know is I loved it right away and took to tennis quickly, but in retrospect, I see how learning to swing was the thing that taught me. Life moves fast, whether you're chasing down a tennis ball or a new investment property. In my experience, the time to take your swing comes in the blink of an eye. My most successful swings were built on practice, determination, and common sense. With those three ingredients, success is inevitable — but not always in the ways you think. You can plan and dream all you want, but life has taught me numerous times that it has its own plan. Sometimes, the plan is good for you; sometimes, it's not. That's why preparation is so necessary. Preparing for success is challenging enough, but sustaining preparedness is even more difficult. Once you've reached initial success, that's the time to double down on determination. Make it your practice to direct your energy efficiently. Use the common sense God gave you and your family instilled in you to handle your success humbly and responsibly.

Ban Nguyen

My father was the first to teach me about preparation, but it took me years to fully understand it. Fifty years ago, he taught me the most crucial lesson in preparing for success while he faced the failure of the government he'd faithfully served his whole life. This government appointed him a military magistrate, giving him responsibility, political influence, and a comfortable home for our family. As everything he'd built for us edged toward oblivion, my father devised a plan to start over in a foreign country. I was just a kid in Vietnam trying to figure out how to hit a backhand down the line. Sure, I knew about the war raging throughout my homeland. I was practically born with the war that tore our country apart. But from that chaos, our family eventually found order in the country I now call home. The journey in between and the journey ever since are compounded miracles. I was dealing with adolescence when fate plucked me from my family and flew me halfway around the world without knowing whether I would ever see them again. Then, we started a new life in Tulsa, Oklahoma, of all places.

We survived the chaos, and my family thrived in our new home in the middle of the United States. Without the preparations my father made on my family's behalf for months before the fall of Saigon, the miracle of finding each other in the Philippines less than a week later would never have manifested. At home, he prepared us to take on the world. He not only paved a path of escape to a new place, but he also instilled in us principles to guide us through life's challenges and succeed at whatever we decided to swing at. Those principles laid the foundation

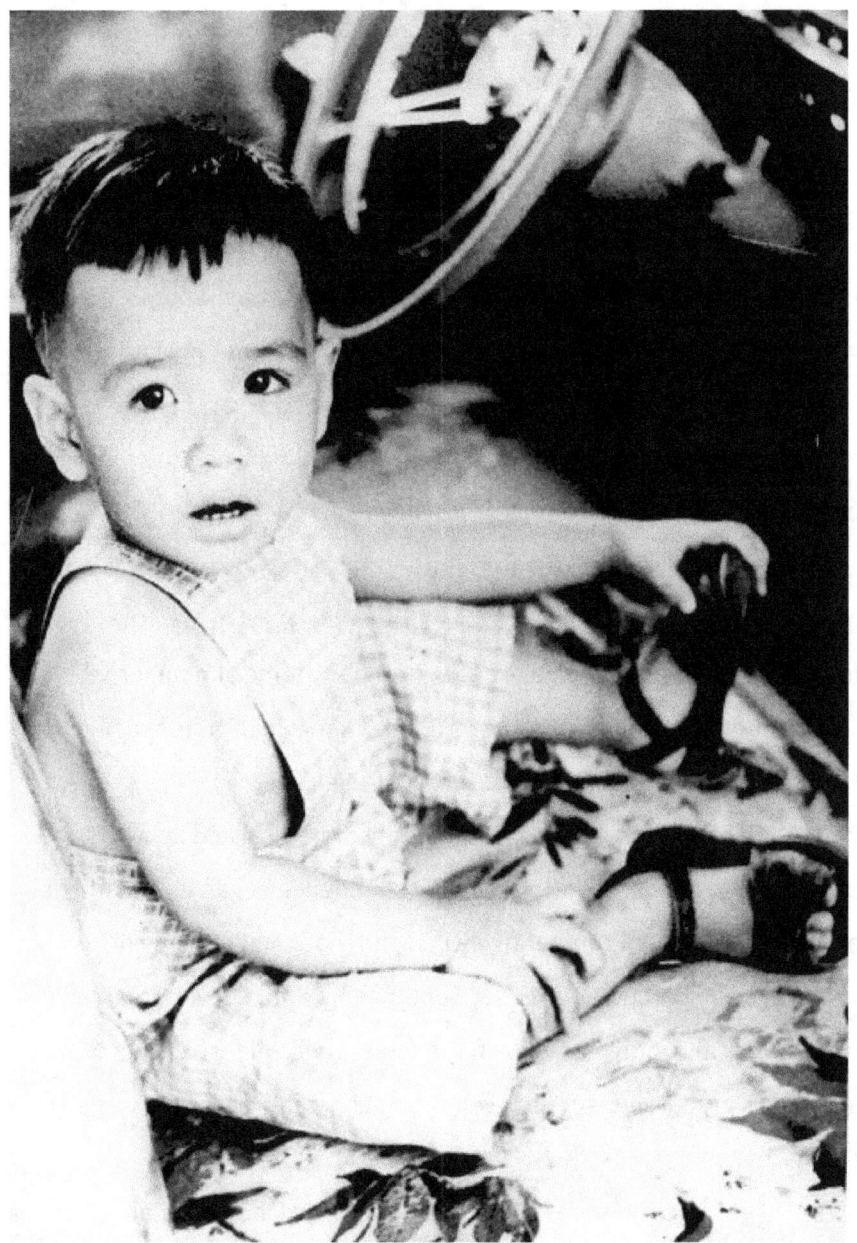

Ban as a toddler

for another miracle. I don't know how else to describe how the youngest boy in the first family of Vietnamese immigrants to arrive in Tulsa, Oklahoma, became the elder statesman of a family of restaurants located throughout the state and beyond its borders.

Now, in my early sixties, I've been thinking about my journey and the people who helped me along the way. It all started at home, and when I got to thinking about it, I realized how important my father's love of sports and my mother's love of gambling played a part in my success... or at least how I approached life. Knowing what and when to swing is crucial, whether playing tennis or placing a bet.

In middle school, the most important swing I learned was with nunchucks. I came to the US without speaking a word of English, which forced me to learn on the go. Navigating a new home and puberty simultaneously was a snap compared to learning English from a bunch of kids in north Tulsa who confused me for Bruce Lee!

Then, in high school, the tennis my father insisted I play started paying off. Accolades followed, and my confidence began to blossom. I also learned to swim competitively in high school and took my first swing at work. Busing tables as a kid at Peppe's Villa Capri, I never dreamed I would work my entire adult life in the food service industry. But my time at Peppe's prepared me for it, even though I had my eyes on college and a computer career.

I got into the social swing in Stillwater, Oklahoma. I learned about liquid courage, Orange pride, and fraternity life. I left Oklahoma State University in 1980, betting on the computer industry, only to wind up working at a restaurant, where I was slinging eggs. I hit it out of the park when I swung at love. Listen, I know there is a rumor floating around out there that my wife, Yen, rejected me the first time I asked her out on a date, but I am here to set the record straight: That's fake news! When Yen and I met, not only did I find a wife, partner, and mother for my children, but she also introduced me to my business mentor. Her parents, Mr. Loc Le and his wife, Kim, bought a small diner in 1980. By the time Yen and I were married, Jimmy's Egg was about ready to expand. Watching Loc and Kim take their swing at Jimmy's Egg and helping it blossom and grow across seven states has been a privilege and an honor. Loc and Kim allowed me to take my swings as a businessman. Not all of them connected, but I'm very proud of my batting average in business. It's an average I'm still working to improve every day.

I'm working on a whole new swing when I'm not working on business. Sure, I still enjoy swinging a tennis racket, but age and a balky back won't allow me to compete the way I enjoy. So I did what every other self-respecting businessman around the world does: I took up golf! Chasing this new swing has forged new friendships and afforded me the opportunity to travel around the world and play at some of the greatest golf courses you can imagine. Thanks to business, golf, and grandfatherhood, I'm still swinging!

This book was inspired by and for my family. When my father got older, he wrote a book about his life, travels, and adventures. He wrote it for his family. He shared it with us all, but not with the rest of the world.

This book is dedicated to my wife, Yen; my oldest son, James, who is CFO of Jimmy's Egg, his wife, Brandi, and their son Mason; my middle son, Khoi, and his wife, Julie, who are both architects; and my daughter

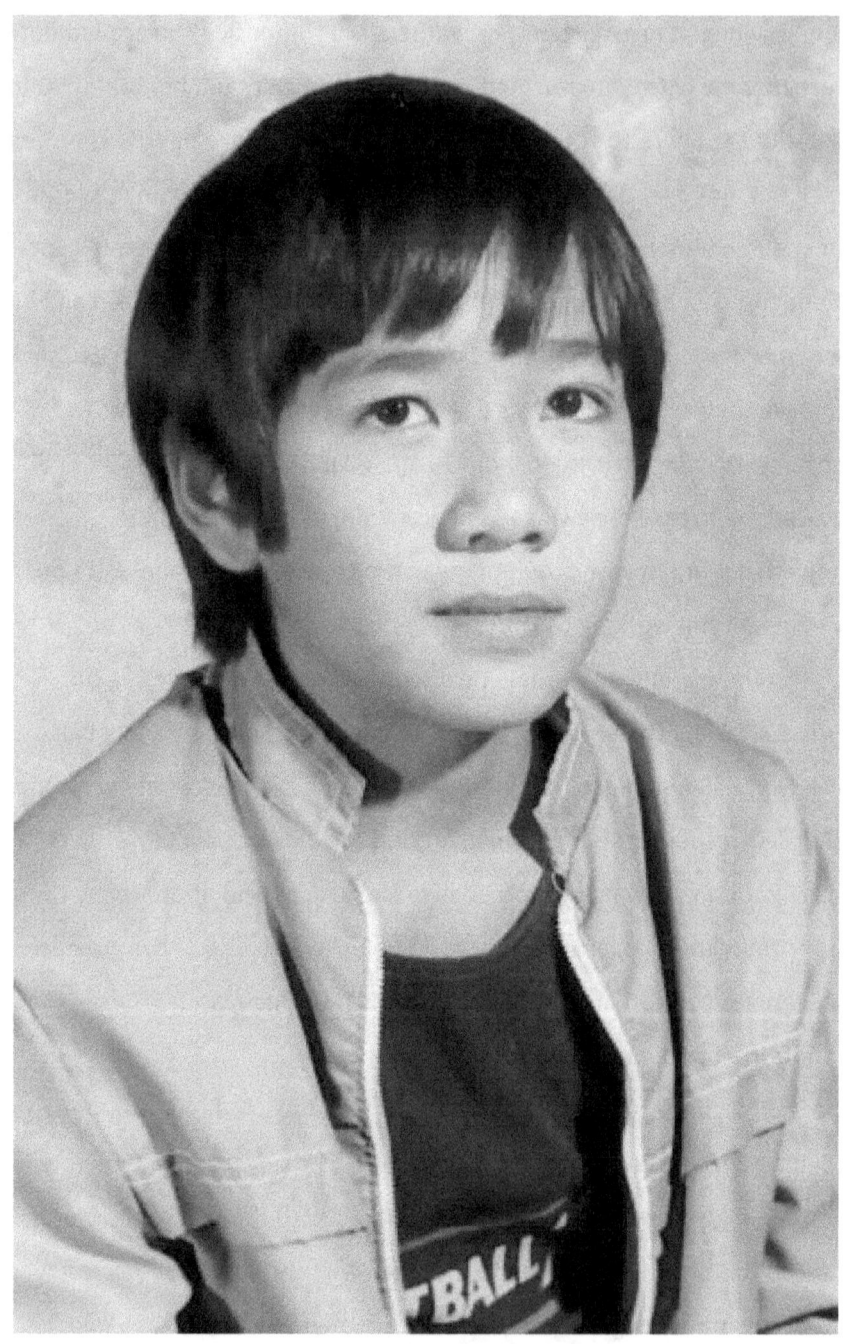

Ban's 8th-grade school photo

Pauline, who is the COO of Jimmy's Egg. I'm so proud of all their many achievements and accomplishments. I hope the joy they've given me in my life is reflected in these pages, and I hope what's in these pages offers context about who they are and where they came from.

We are a family of Vietnamese Americans by fate. I came here as a refugee half a century ago, with 130,000 others starting in 1975. Because I came to the United States as a boy, half my upbringing was under the red, white, and blue banner. Today, I think I'm more American than Vietnamese and more Okie from Muskogee than anything else. But in my mind, I still think in Vietnamese. I find value in that binary. The refugees who came to this country fifty years ago have had a profoundly positive impact on American culture. I'm just as proud to call myself a refugee as I am an American. My American story is founded on adapting to our conditions. Looking back today, I am so proud of the footprint the refugee class I came from has left on our new home. I'm proud to be a Vietnamese American.

Helping grow Jimmy's Egg diners all over the country while raising a family, I've developed the three Ds. I live by this credo and preach it all the time. The first D is for desire, the second for dreams, and the third for dissatisfaction. Desire is pretty obvious. Accomplishing any goal starts with desire, whether to make money, set a record, or maybe write a book, right? The first D is about getting your hands dirty, perhaps even getting a little blood on your nose. Once you get dirty and build a work ethic, you dream. You set some goals. That's what dreams are about. Finally, the third D stands for dissatisfied and is the most difficult D once you've had some success. It's easy to get so used to celebrating your wins that you become complacent, maybe even a little depressed. You start to feel like you don't want anymore. That's when it becomes easy to slow down. The work ethic begins to slip a little bit. Next thing you know, you're falling off a cliff! The lesson is that you should leave room to improve and grow regardless of your level. It's no different than wanting to take that four handicap down to zero. I've preached this principle to my kids for years.

The story I have to share is mine, as best I can remember, but I have seven siblings who might remember some of the events differently. I did my best to get the details right. Sitting down to recount everything that happened, the people I met, and the swings I've taken, one word kept coming to mind: miraculous. How in the hell does a thirteen-year-old kid who doesn't speak English grow up to become president of a restaurant chain responsible for cracking almost 10 million eggs a year? It must be a miracle, right? Maybe, but the bigger miracle might be how that same kid wrote a book fifty years later without his English ever getting much better!

Keep reading, and you can decide.

One

Tennis Anyone?

One of the most important things my father did for me when I was a boy was to put a tennis racket in my hand. My father loved tennis, but loved competition and chasing victory even more than tennis. Whether on a tennis court, at a horse racing track, or in life, it didn't matter. He taught us, in actions more than words, that a strong competitive spirit was crucial to winning in life. When it came to tennis or almost anything else, my father was unafraid to pit us kids against each other. However, he also insisted we teach each other. At least my older siblings had to teach. Because I was the youngest, I mostly learned! But it's true: if I came to my father asking for help playing tennis, he would send me to my older brothers, who were only interested in improving themselves. Their determination became my determination, and I learned how to swing a tennis racket properly. I had no fancy instructors; I was entirely self-taught, learning from lessons my big brothers either showed me or inflicted on me. We all benefited, and the newspaper clippings prove it.

One of the secrets to the success of Jimmy's Egg is prioritizing which responsibilities to take on and which to outsource. One thing that

Cercle Sportif Saigonnais (Sai Gon Sport Circle Club) 1973

might surprise people is that we handle the accounting for our stores from our homes. We do it old-school. Each store's financial records are kept in a separate three-ring binder. Each binder is placed in a cart where we store all the records. That cart full of binders sits right next to my desk in the home office. From there, I can look out the window and see my front yard. In that office, I keep many of my most cherished possessions. No, not the McLaren! I'm talking about items that remind me of the path from Cam Ranh Bay in Vietnam to the US and what inspires me to succeed as CEO of Jimmy's Egg. Pictures of family hang on the walls, special bottles are kept on a shelf in the walk-in closet, and all the trophies I earned starting at a young age loom over the entire office. I won most of the hardware playing tennis, the sport my father chose for my brothers and me.

My father joined the Vietnamese military as a young man and advanced rapidly over the years, gaining significant social advantages. He recognized the value of tennis when a Davis Cup exhibition came to Vietnam in 1969. Stan Smith, Arthur Ashe, and Bob Lutz came to town, and my father served as a chair umpire. My older brothers were ball boys. Golf was nonexistent in Vietnam then, and tennis was very popular worldwide, especially among the French, who had occupied my home country for so long. My father's role in the Vietnamese government helped him recognize the popularity and social significance of tennis. My father was wise enough to realize that if tennis had a future in Vietnam, then his sons needed a future in tennis. He groomed us to be athletes. He told us we wouldn't play any music; we were to concentrate on competing in sports. The number one sport he had in mind was tennis.

11

Country site in Cam Ranh Bay, with Dad (front left), Ban (front right),
Trang (back center), and Dad's two bodyguards (1968)

Because of my father, my two older brothers, An and Ross, were
very accomplished when our family eventually came to the United States.
Neither became a Davis Cup champion nor has Vietnam produced a world
champion, but tennis did play a pivotal role in my family's future. An and
Ross earned tennis scholarships to Baker University in Baldwin City,
Kansas. I played all through high school and for my fraternity at Oklahoma
State University. But that's getting ahead of the story.

As I mentioned, tennis was the family sport, according to my
father, who was a self-made man. Born in Nam Dinh, a province
in northern Vietnam's Red River Delta region, my father, Bang Dinh,
became an orphan at the age of fourteen. He never discussed his military

High School tennis duel (1980)

life with me, but my mother shared the stories with me when I got older.

He was the youngest child in his family. His father was very old when he was born and died not long after. My father never graduated from high school, advancing no further than the eighth grade. He went off to fight with Ho Chi Minh at age fourteen to fight the French, but the enemy captured him. He was strung up and tortured before a French commander took him in and made him his houseboy. That's where my father learned French. This military commander falsified the paperwork that helped my dad gain admission to the Dalat Military Academy, where he graduated third in his class. My father was in the fifth class of the academy after it was re-established in 1954 by President Ngo Dinh Diem. In 1959, he was promoted to major and assigned as military mayor of Ban Me Thuot.

Most of my memories of family life in Vietnam came from when he served as a military magistrate in charge of Cam Ranh Bay. It's a place with a rich military history. In 1965, the US military built a vast complex, including a supply base and airfields, over much of the 100-square-mile peninsula where we lived. During World War II, Japanese forces seized it, then withdrew in 1945. In 1972, while we were living in Cam Ranh Bay, it was turned back over to the South Vietnamese military. There, we lived in an urban compound near the city center, across the street from a horse racing track and not far from Chinatown. Every weekend, my mother and father took the family to the track because gambling is very popular in Vietnamese culture, no matter whether you're rich or poor.

Gambling is up there, almost with religion and fortune-telling. (In my family, maybe a little bit higher!) For a thirteen-year-old, I had it pretty

Swinging and Slinging

Ban (front) at the Saigon racetrack, with Mom (standing) and Grandpa to his mom's right (1969)

good. We lived in a wealthy area and owned three cars and a motorcycle.

I was still riding my bicycle, chased by a dog named Bobby. It was comfortable from 1967 until the spring of 1975. That's the place I remember most, hosting family during the holidays, playing with my brothers and sisters, and honing my tennis swing.

Meanwhile, my mother and father hosted dignitaries like General William Westmoreland, Secretary of Defense Robert MacNamara, and Vice President Spiro Agnew. How does an orphan from northern Vietnam play host to VIPs from the US in southern Vietnam? He married up!

15

Ban Nguyen

Unlike my father, my mother, Khue Van, came from an affluent family in Hanoi. Raised like a debutante in the US, she learned all the formal dances, how to walk properly, and exhibit proper manners. But underneath it all, Mom was a rebel. She lost her mother early, and then her family lost everything during the Japanese occupation of Hanoi during World War II. Even after her father lost his wealth, he was able to retain the family home and maintain his social standing. Among his favorite pastimes was playing mahjong with friends. One of his regular opponents was driven to the house by a young, confident chauffeur—confident enough to wander through the gardens while his boss was off in the main house playing.

A pretty, young gardener tending to the flowers caught the driver's eye, so he approached her, struck up a conversation, and eventually asked her out. The problem was that she was no gardener. She was my mother, Khue Van. She loved tending the garden and had no problem overstepping social boundaries. She said yes. Her answer didn't fit my grandfather's plans, but he must have recognized my father's ambitions. My parents were married for fifty-eight years and raised eight children—four boys and four girls. I was the youngest boy, the second youngest overall. My sister, Trang, was the youngest. No matter where we fell on the timeline, my father was determined to raise only alphas. My siblings would attest to that.

Whenever I accomplished something good, I would run to my father to brag or seek approval. Instead of patting me on the head or something like that, he would always point towards my brothers and sisters, "Well, look at what your sister has done," or "Look at what your

16

Lunar New Year photo, from oldest to youngest: Ong Ngoai, Dad, Mom,
Dung, Tuan, Mai, An, Nguyen (Ross), Lien, Ban, and Trang

brothers have done." He wasn't satisfied with reaching one goal and
wasn't about to let us be satisfied so easily.

We had a strict upbringing based on military principles and old-
school Vietnamese culture. That is to say, the boys got preferential
treatment. Asian cultures have historically prioritized sons. This adage
goes with old, conservative ideas about men being the breadwinners, so
daughters didn't get the same attention. On top of this, my parents,
especially my mom, were very superstitious. They both believed in
fortune tellers, so my dad brought one to our house to meet my brothers
and me and tell my parents what kind of future he saw for us. That turned
out to be one of the most important meetings of my life, and I didn't even
know it was happening. This fortune teller told my parents that their

oldest son would fight the good fight throughout life, trying and succeeding at many things, but would likely switch careers frequently. The seer told my parents their second son would wear a white coat for most of his life. So, now my parents are excited. They're thinking of the medical field, and he'd be a doctor for sure! Then he tells them the third son would follow in his father's footsteps. He was going to be a military man.

As for me, the fortune teller predicted I would be a leader, no matter the field or endeavor. I hate to say it, but those predictions were remarkably prophetic. My oldest brother, Tuan's, career began as soon as we arrived in Tulsa. He had already finished high school, so when we got settled in, he had to go straight to work to help my father support the family. Since then, his career has included several industries, including restaurants. He had a very popular all-you-can-eat buffet in Tulsa. My brother, An, never became a doctor. Still, he has worked his whole life in hospitals. Ross is retired from the US Army, where he served as a Lieutenant Colonel, and is now Executive Director of the Vietnamese American Uniformed Service Association.

As for me, I'm currently the Chief Executive Officer of Jimmy's Egg Incorporated and captain of the Vietnam United men's golf team. That's right, golf, not tennis! I had to learn an entirely different kind of swing in middle age, but since I've been learning to swing since I was old enough to walk, I could pick it up, using the same powers of observation and adaptation I used to create a tennis swing. Watching my older brothers, who were more interested in punishing me on the court than teaching me anything, was the perfect training ground. I observed them. I emulated their movements and the way they swung their rackets. Eventually, I had a swing of my own. They taught me whether they meant to or not.

The key to the swing is repetition. The only way to develop consistency in anything is through repetition. It's no different with tennis or golf. If you can make consistent, good contact, repeat it. Control and confidence follow, and then you can make tweaks. I never had any fancy instructors like you see now. I never attended tennis camps, but my self-taught swing took me a long way. That approach has served me well in both business and life. Life has taught me the importance of preparation in achieving success. Throw preparation before desire and repetition, and you've got an unbeatable formula. My first real lesson in preparation came without my knowledge, and my father gave it as our country was crumbling.

In the spring of 1975, I was thirteen years old, happy to spend my days playing tennis or being chased on my bike by Bobby the German Shepherd. Then, one fateful day, my mother and father gathered the whole family to tell us what the rest of the world knew: the war was against our side. My father said that if anything happened, he'd send the two youngest children to live with a family from the US to ensure the Nguyen line would continue.

An American military officer had already convinced my parents that the war was not going to end well for the South. My father was planning to stay and fight, but Mr. Boyce planned to get us all out of the country. What I didn't know at the time was that my father had made these plans months before. Everything in the world around me and my family was starting to move very fast. I couldn't quite understand it all as a kid, but I knew a war was happening in my home country. I was barely walking when the war began. I later learned that those times my father sent me to my brothers for tennis advice weren't just because he thought it was up to us to help each other improve. It was because he was preparing for the family's escape. Sure, it was a gamble, but gambling was practically sacred in our household. That's probably why I still love going to Las Vegas every chance I get; it reminds me of my mother, who loved visiting Las Vegas to play Three Card Poker and Pai Gow. And why not? Gambling might've saved us all. Besides taking the family to the local racecourse on weekends, my mother went almost daily. That's where they met Mr. Edward Boyce of Colorado Springs, Colorado, who would eventually set the stage for my family's escape from Vietnam. Gambling on horses was a national pastime in Vietnam, and it wasn't uncommon for people to go to the little local track in the middle of the day. Mr. Boyce was a US military colonel, who we would later learn was also an agent for the Central Intelligence Agency. My mother and father were pretty successful gamblers, but Mr. Boyce's friendship was undoubtedly the most valuable thing they ever won at that track.

Planning began in December 1974. Then, late one April afternoon, the plot thickened. My parents gathered the family to tell us my sister, Trang, and I were going with Mr. Boyce and his wife, Pat. The rest of the family would catch up with us in the Philippines if they were able to get out at all. When Trang and I said goodbye to our mother, father, and siblings that evening, there was no guarantee we would see any of them ever again. I remember the whole family sitting around and Bobby, too, just looking at each other in disbelief. My mother packed me a small duffle bag that included a few clothes but, more importantly, two hundred dollars in cash and an ounce of gold. Having that stuff made me so nervous. I didn't even reach into that bag for a change of clothes. I wore the same pair of bell bottoms for the next week—a week that began in the trunk of the Boyce's car.

We started to get in the back seat, but they told us to jump in the trunk instead. My sister is tough. I'm even scared of her today because she's a bigger alpha than me! That night, she acted cool, but I was terrified and crying like a baby! I didn't understand any of it. I remember Mr. Boyce telling my sister and me to get in the trunk, and we did what he said. We got in that trunk. We went through what I could tell were at least two security checkpoints. Then, the trunk popped open at the last stop, and we were right there in front of this big old airplane. Mr. Boyce picked us up and handed us off to his wife, who was right at the door, and she put us on the plane. There must've been four hundred Vietnamese on that plane. We didn't know any of them. All we knew for sure was how unsure everything was.

Landing in the Philippines didn't make us kids feel any more secure. There, authorities whisked us to a Filipino military base, Clark Air Base, where we stayed in huge army barracks filled with cots. There was no privacy, familiar faces, certainty, or security. They lined us all up and told us to find a spot. Mrs. Boyce, who was the loveliest lady, stayed with us. Her daughter, Carol, bunked with us that whole week, too. For the first two days, crying was about all I did. I couldn't stop crying. My sister and I couldn't even talk because we wanted to know what was happening. I was so terrified when it was time to shower that I made my sister come and watch me. You know you're scared if you ask your sister to stand guard while you shower!

We eventually started to meet other kids. I remember kicking a soccer ball around with them. Exactly seven days after saying goodbye to our family and hello to a life of chaos, order was restored. My sister and I left on April 20, 1975. It was a Sunday. Shortly after we'd had dinner the following Sunday, I saw my mother and father approaching us with the rest of the family behind them. Mr. Boyce had convinced my father to buy airline tickets to a destination they had no intention of going to. Once the family was at the airport, Mr. Boyce guided them to the American side, where they got a flight to Clark Air Base. While we were reunited, Mrs. Boyce packed up our stuff. I didn't understand all the ramifications of what was happening, but when I saw that my belongings were packed, I went with my family. The first thing I remember doing was digging that money out of my duffel bag and finding the valuables. I handed my mom the two hundred dollars and the ounce of gold.

"That's yours," I told her. "I don't want it. Done!"

My family and I were on a plane headed for Guam the same night. Our destination was Wake Island, a coral atoll in Micronesia that Pan-American Airways used as a stopover for trans-Pacific flights before the Boeing 747 made it moot. The US Air Force converted it into a base in 1972. Wake Island had simple barracks—four walls made of concrete surrounding a bunch of bunk beds. Our family got bunks in a corner together. I was too young to know we were a part of Operation New Life. All I knew was that I was back with my family and planned to follow where they went.

Three days after we arrived, right around suppertime, we got the news that Saigon had fallen. No one was surprised, but everyone was heartbroken. There was no going home. Our processing was over just a couple of days later. That put us on an airplane to the United States, landing at Fort Chaffee in Arkansas, where thousands of Vietnamese refugees would follow.

Lunar New Year, Ban and sister Trang (1973)

Fort Chaffee was a brutal and humbling camp. The barracks were massive and stark. No more than eight or nine families would occupy a barracks, but everyone had bunk beds to share in a wide-open space. There was no privacy or intimacy at all. I remember they piled donated clothes around the barracks for people to go and pick out shoes or a shirt—whatever they could find. Remember that many people didn't have time to pack—just the clothes on their backs. My father was no stranger to this environment, given his upbringing, but he was also naturally wily and well-educated, thanks to his French heritage. He recognized that Fort Chaffee's living conditions were barely above those of a prison or concentration camp. He spoke English, French, and Vietnamese and underwent military training at Fort Leavenworth, Kansas, and Fort Knox, Kentucky.

That prepared him for leadership and taught him its value. At Fort Chaffee, he immediately volunteered with the officers at the base to help register refugees. That put him in a position to recognize opportunities. The one he found for our family came in a big, white Cadillac sedan.

Earl A. Stehle rolled into Fort Chaffee with his wife, Christine, in that big, white Cadillac, looking for opportunity. What that opportunity was is a matter of debate. According to an article in the *Tulsa World* written by Janet Macklin in 1975, the intention was "to help out." However, our first real lesson in American capitalism came from Mr. and Mrs. Stehle, who goodheartedly capitalized on my family's plight. Namely, to operate a Mobil service station they owned in north Tulsa for next to nothing. Nevertheless, it was a chance to leave Fort Chaffee right away. Our other options were waiting for sponsorship from the Boyces in

Colorado Springs or my father's relative, who had married an American advisor living in Washington, D.C.

Living at Fort Chafee was controlled chaos. Barely controlled. My father knew we needed to leave there as soon as possible, even if it meant rolling the dice on a guy named Earl and living in Tulsa time.

Ban with the family car in the garage on Lunar New Year (1972)

Two

Nunchucks

The nunchaku has many names: dual–section sticks, chain sticks, chuka sticks, and nunchucks. The traditional East Asian martial arts weapon is made of two sticks connected at their ends by a short metal chain or rope. Before moving to Tulsa, Oklahoma, all I knew about nunchucks was how cool they looked when Bruce Lee used them in movies like *Fist of Fury* in 1972 and again in *Enter the Dragon* in 1973. When my family arrived in Tulsa, those two movies were cult classics, playing at drive-ins and midnight movies nationwide. I knew all about Bruce Lee, but I never dreamed how much he would help and hurt me in junior high school.

When Earl and Christine Stehle first moved my entire family from Fort Chaffee to Tulsa in a two-door sedan pulling a U-Haul, we spent a brief time living with them in their home. Earl's Mobil gas station wasn't far away, and Earl had the idea that my dad, my brothers, and I would run the station for him. No problem. We were happy about the opportunity. Working in a gas station might seem like a pretty straightforward, simple job today, but in 1975, gas stations looked nothing like the pay-at-the-pump mega stations we see today from QuikTrip, 7-Eleven, and Buc-ee's.

Before the 1960s, self-service was rare thanks to state fire codes. California had the first self-serve pumps in the late 1940s. Still, the first remote-access self-service gasoline pumps were activated at a convenience store in Colorado in the summer of 1964. Today, full-service stations are extremely rare. As you can probably guess, self-service was growing exponentially in 1975, but there were still plenty of full-service stations around at that time. The Stehle's Mobil station was among them. For the first three to four months in town, the Nguyen brothers would get up every morning to have breakfast with the Stehle family, and after we were done, it was straight over to the gas station. We really helped the business thanks to my father's media savvy.

We came to Tulsa when gasoline was on everyone's mind. The decade was marked by an energy crisis, including a series of Saudi embargoes contributing to skyrocketing inflation. In 1975, waiting in line to get gasoline became routine. Gas rationing based on whether your license plate ended in an odd or even number became routine. Some stations posted red or green flags to indicate whether they had gas. The energy crisis was the reason behind the adoption of a 55-mph federal speed limit. With people used to waiting in line for gas, my father had an idea to turn our line into the longest one. His background in politics gave him a certain amount of media savvy. He knew there had been stories written about Vietnamese immigrants in the local newspaper because that's how the Stehles found us in the first place. So, my father had the idea to notify the local media that Tulsa's first family of Vietnamese refugees had arrived, and we were running a Mobil gas station. My family briefly became local celebrities thanks to *Tulsa World* and the local TV

Ban's dad and mom at his older sister, Lien's, wedding (1982)

stations. Sure, it felt a little like being zoo animals because, in pre-Internet Tulsa, the only Vietnamese people it's residence had ever seen were on the news, usually in terrible distress, whether fighting for or against the US military.

Either way, there was enough curiosity about us in Tulsa that people lined up for blocks to get gas from Stehle's gas station. The move turned out to be a boon for Mr. Stehle, but it opened my family's eyes to local generosity. We saw the Oklahoma Standard in action for the first time. The coverage made it clear that we'd come to Tulsa with what we could carry. That was the first time I saw Oklahoma hospitality and charity up close and personal. People filled a bucket with cash donations, while others dropped off dry goods and miscellaneous items. The home we were saving toward would eventually include furniture donated during that time. One gentleman handed over the title and keys to an old Ford Falcon, which my dad happily accepted. My family has been truly fortunate not to need that kind of help since, but I've seen Oklahoma step up for its neighbors many times over the years after deadly tornadoes, floods, and fires, which are all too common in Oklahoma. That kindness has never been forgotten, and when a domestic terrorist bombed the Alfred P Murrah federal building, I saw how Oklahoma takes care of its own and joined the cause. I remember working with local Oklahoma City disc jockeys, Jack and Ron, to deliver 30 or 40 breakfasts daily to our emergency response workers for a week following the catastrophe. We joined similar efforts after the May 3 tornado. In retrospect, I see how Tulsa made my family one of its own during that spell, almost like an initiation. More would follow for us, but that initiation helped us build a home in North Tulsa. All of it helped rebuild my family's prospects and remains an active generosity that resonates in my family history to this day.

Probably the worst part about those early days staying with the Stehle family was breakfast. Some of us were sleeping in the house, and some were sleeping in a room above the attic, but we were all eating together. First, understand that we came from a culture that didn't include a traditional breakfast. In Vietnam, the morning meal might be fruit, rice, or a French pastry. There wasn't a lot of emphasis on breakfast. So, when Mrs. Stehle kindly got up to make us a meal before we went to work every morning, we were confused but thankful. Obviously, I came around on breakfast—I operated a chain of restaurants that relied on the very same foods I was unfamiliar with then—but Mrs. Stehle made one dish I still can't eat to this day: oatmeal. I had never heard of oatmeal, and I hated it immediately. Still do. To this day, you won't catch me eating oatmeal. Even at Jimmy's Egg, we've got grits but no oatmeal! At the time, though, we were happy to be together with a roof over our heads and anything to eat, even if it was disgusting oatmeal!

My father knew he eventually had to get out from under the servitude we were giving Earl Stehle for his initial grace. For a little while, we stayed in the Stehle home, located in a neighborhood of homes built in the 1920s and 1930s. The houses were quaint but rundown. We were just happy to have options. The house next door to the Stehle's was for rent, but not for long after my parents found out. We moved into the new place and quickly learned our new landlord's mother had lived in the house across the street before we came to town. After that first summer, my father approached the landlord about buying the vacant house. Our neighborhood was probably among the worst in Tulsa, but we were in no position to be picky. So, my dad approached the landlord about buying the house, and I recall the man asking for around $ 9,000. Can you imagine a house for $9000? Even back then, that wasn't very much. The price was less a reflection of the late 1970s economy than how rough north Tulsa was in those days and the house's state of disrepair. My father paid for the house in cash, and our family went to work on it ourselves to renovate it. Little by little, we made the house at 1141 N. Cheyenne into a home. My parents lived there long after all of us kids graduated and left for college. Long after my parents sold it, our old neighborhood experienced a renaissance. Now, it's on the National Register of Historic Neighborhoods.

For me, the most important thing about moving was getting away from Mrs. Stehle's oatmeal and in front of my mother's delicious cooking. My mother embodied beauty and grace, but never more so than when in her kitchen kingdom. I loved my mother's cooking so much that my wife, Yen, agreed to spend a couple of weeks living with us and learning my mom's recipes before we married! Cooking was my mother's greatest joy because it meant being surrounded by family. For her family, she loved to showcase her culinary skills by building elaborate feasts of traditional Vietnamese cuisine. Mom knew everyone's favorite dish and would promise them weeks in advance of their birthday. My only complaint was that three of us had birthdays in early June, and I was the youngest, so my favorites got lost! But even somebody else's favorite was the best thing I could eat in those days.

Ban Nguyen

Having a place of our own to live was great, and getting out of oatmeal and into Mom's food was amazing, but worse challenges than oatmeal awaited me at school. I arrived old enough to enter eighth grade as the school year was winding down. At that time, I had zero command of the English language. Adolescence is difficult enough; I had to face mine in a place where literally nobody looked like me, that I wasn't related to, and I didn't speak the language. What saved me was the tennis swing and the mathematics I learned in Vietnam. My homemade tennis swing performed well in the US, and despite not learning English at Vietnamese schools, I learned math that eighth graders in Tulsa had not yet been taught. I was working on trigonometry-level math by then in Vietnam, so all the math they were doing in Tulsa was easy. That caught the attention of one counselor, who made it her responsibility to pick me up before school every morning and drive me to James Madison Junior High School, a lower-income school, where I was received terribly. Even so, I was relieved when summer arrived. I didn't care that I spent that first summer cleaning windshields. All I knew was I didn't have to try reading or writing in English!

My experience at James Madison was positive, which made returning to school a little less imposing. However, when I learned my school would be Roosevelt Junior High School instead, I was deflated. Roosevelt had a terrible reputation at the time. The student body consisted of all students from low-income families. The kids I went to school with in the mid-1970s all came from poor, primarily black families. All the kids I went to school with had a collective chip on their shoulders, pushed around plenty by life. These kids would not suffer fools or any kids

32

with perceived weaknesses. My English wasn't just a perceived weakness. Sure, my English improved that summer, but only from nonexistent to terrible. I mean, really terrible. Speaking was hard enough, but learning to read a new language was even harder. Somehow, I made the honor roll at Roosevelt Junior High School, which is more an indication of the school than a measure of my studiousness. Poor English skills made class difficult, but my long hair, different skin color, and communication struggles became a magnet for the attention of bullies.

My tennis swing benefited my long-term future, but I had to learn a whole new swing to survive in the short term at Roosevelt. The worldwide superstardom of Bruce Lee directly affected my prospects in middle school. Because he was the only person of Asian heritage most folks in Tulsa had ever seen, "Bruce Lee" became my nickname to the bullies. Once I reached my limit with them, I decided to give them a dose of Bruce Lee—namely, his weapon of choice on the silver screen. Before I ever got to Tulsa, I knew all about Bruce Lee, but I never thought of myself as someone people would mistake for him. We were of different nationalities, spoke different languages, and looked nothing alike. Believe me, I would've loved to look like Bruce Lee! So, I was pretty confused when kids started calling me by his name. The real test came in gym class, though. Gym class was always the worst place for bullying. You get a bunch of scared adolescent boys isolated away from faculty, and their fears and insecurities will manifest into hostility. My English was terrible, but I understood what was going on when people started pulling my hair, kicking me from behind, and calling me names. Pretty soon, I ended up with a busted lip here and a bloody nose there. I was too ashamed to tell anyone what was happening, especially at home. Finally, after one guy knocked me down, stood on top of me, and announced, "I just kicked Bruce Lee's ass," I decided if it was Bruce Lee they wanted, it was Bruce Lee they were going to get.

I spent the next month plotting and practicing. I didn't have revenge in mind, but I was done taking the abuse. The first thing I did was cut a broomstick into sections. Then, I drilled holes in two sections and bound them together with a small chain to create a set of homemade nunchucks. Then I practiced. There were no YouTube videos to follow along with in those days; I had to practice by feel. Just as with the tennis swing, I watched to learn and experimented to improve. It took me several weeks, but I took my time because it was clear the only way to escape this tyranny was by force. I snuck the nunchucks to school and hid them in my gym locker. Sure enough, one day, the same three guys who liked picking on me the most stepped up with venom in their eyes. I was ready. I went nuts on them, and from that day on, nobody messed with me. In fact, from that day on, it made me a lot of friends. Those bullies never gave me trouble again. I remember their names clearly; even though this is my story, I won't embarrass them. But I will tell you those homemade nunchucks still hang among my most treasured trophies, right next to an old tennis racket.

Reflecting on that time, it's easy to see how it prepared me to survive and flourish in this country. It was rough, but it toughened me up in the right ways. It was a good lesson about how coping with challenges

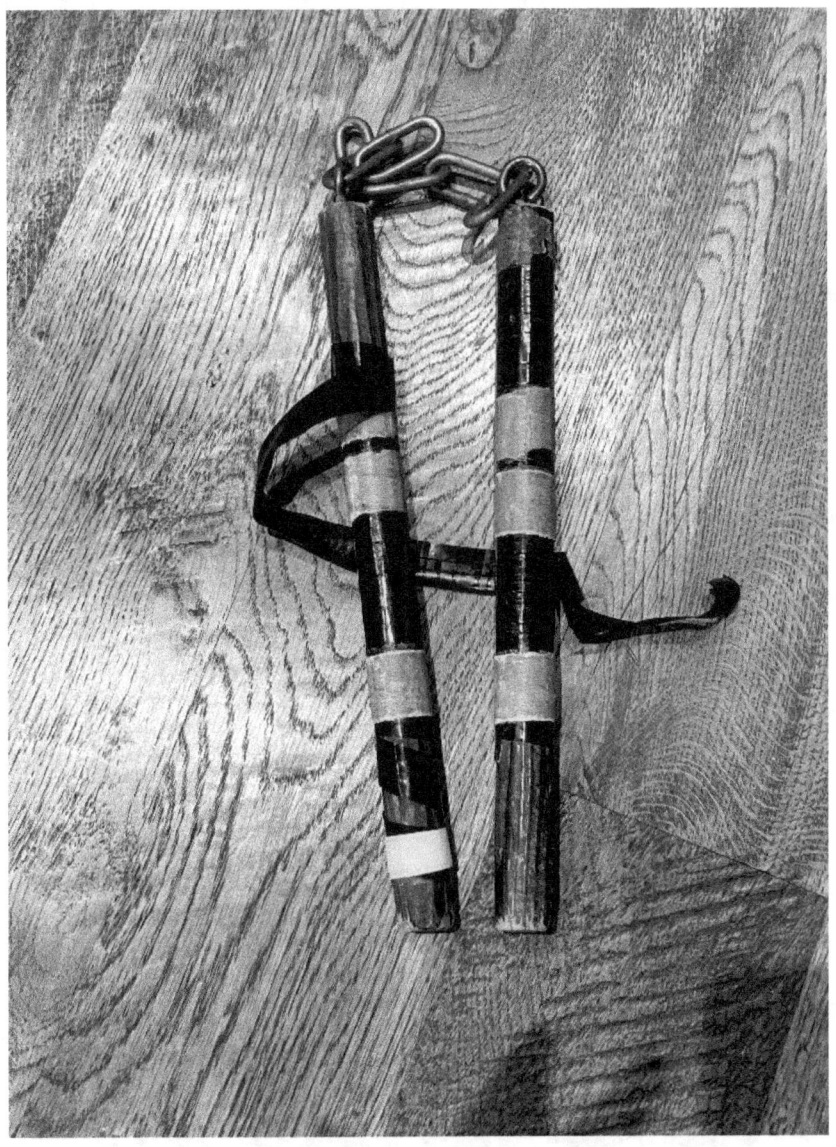

Ban's handmade nunchucks from a broomstick

shapes a person and a reminder of how tough life can be. Bullies exist in every walk of life, but the alpha attitude my father raised me with prepared me for them. I never would've made those nunchucks if it hadn't. The bullies were mere confirmations that my upbringing would play well in the States—graduating with minimal, practical English skills with a lesson in negotiation. Without my tennis swing and swimming strokes, I might never have been able to take a swing at college.

Ban holding the nunchucks he handcrafted in school

Three

Swing Shift

Gambling has been a big part of my life since I was born. My family loves the ponies, mahjong, and any excuse to visit Vegas. We beat long odds, making it from Saigon to Tulsa, Oklahoma, in less than sixty days, but probably the longest odds I personally ever beat were getting into college. First, not many kids I went to high school with went to college. Second, those who did *all* spoke better English than I and read and wrote it better. To beat those odds, I had to have an amazing support system. The kind of support system that wouldn't let me wait too long to get started. The kind of support system that expects alpha behavior. Lucky for me, that's precisely the kind of support system I had.

Although I had to hustle through school in the States, education held a great deal of importance for me. In Vietnamese culture, education is a very high priority. Most people, including myself, come from large families that view education as the key to success. My father and oldest brother worked extremely hard when we first arrived in Tulsa to ensure that the rest of us kids graduated from high school and had a chance to attend college. I still owe them both such a debt of gratitude.

37

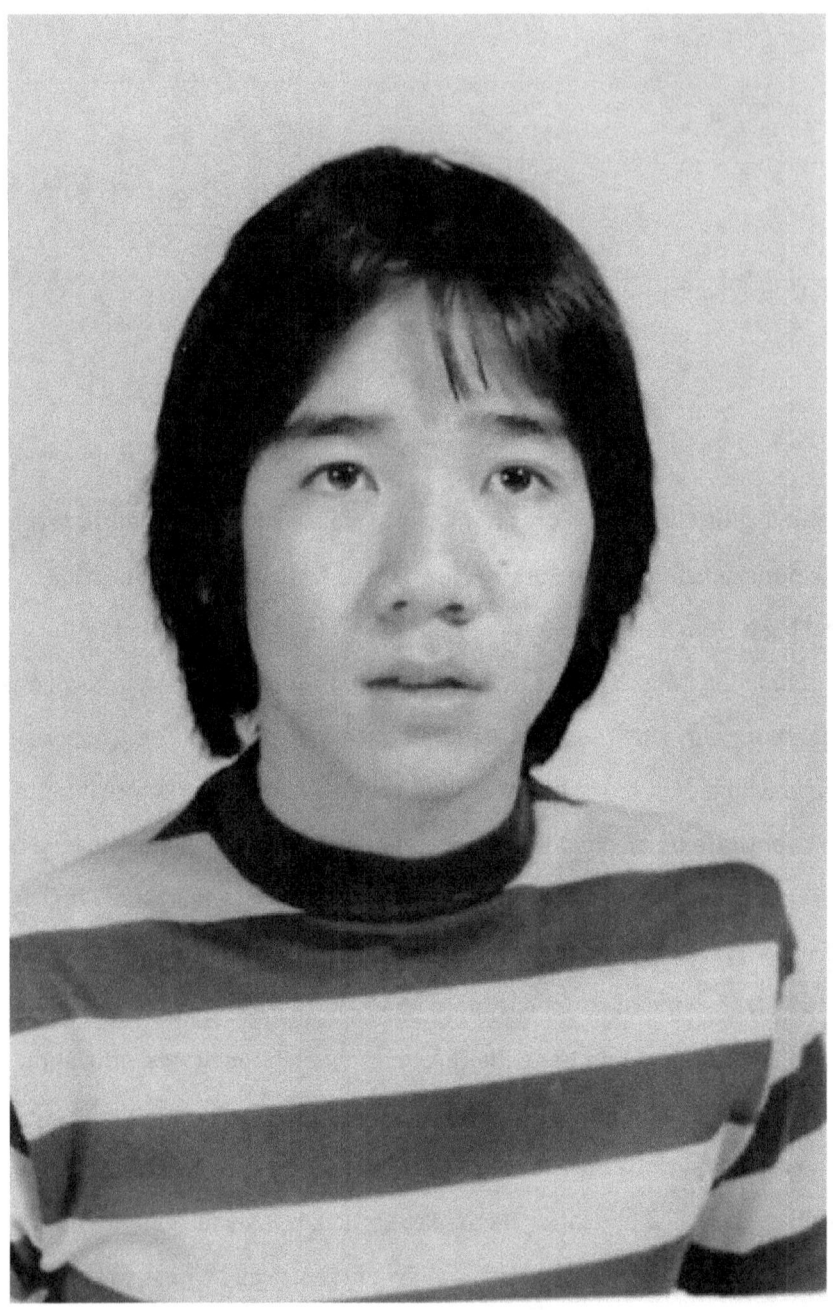

Ban's 10th-grade school photo

Swinging and Slinging

My tennis swing was coming along much better than my English when I got to high school, and I doubled down on athletic extracurriculars by joining the tennis and swim teams at Tulsa Central High School. As I explained in the previous chapter, English grammar and writing skills were the most significant challenges I faced upon arriving in the United States. Thankfully, Vietnam's emphasis on mathematics put me ahead of the curve in that subject, and my father's passion for tennis gave me an extracurricular activity to bring to the market and eventually put on my transcript. The most important thing I had by the time I graduated from Tulsa Central High School in 1980 was confidence. It might've been false confidence, but sometimes that's where the courage to place a bet on long odds comes from. Just like Roosevelt Junior High, Tulsa Central had a reputation for being a tough school. All that did was provide plenty of opportunities to build my self-confidence, as there was no shortage of challenges.

I can't discount the confidence gained from swinging those nunchucks to stand up for myself, but my backhand helped the most. Few things are more satisfying than a good backhand down the line. I hit enough of them to play in college. Even though I didn't accept a scholarship offer after making the All-City Tennis Team at Central, my backhand didn't become a weapon until I was almost done with college. I also made the All-City Swim Team, but I had the opportunity to follow in the footsteps of my two brothers, who attended Baker University in Baldwin, Kansas. But it was a small Baptist school that didn't have the computer program I was looking for at the time, and increasing back pain

Ban Nguyen

Central High School
TULSA, OKLAHOMA
Athletic Letter Award

This certifies that _BAN Nguyen_

has been awarded the **T** Athletic Letter in

SWIMMING

Date _3-8-78_

Head Coach

Athletic Director

Principal

Ban's high school Athletic Letter Award for Swimming

Central High School
TULSA, OKLAHOMA
Athletic Letter Award

This certifies that _Ban Nguyen_

has been awarded the **T** Athletic Letter in

TENNIS

Date _May 5, 1978_

Head Coach

Athletic Director

Principal

Ban's high school Athletic Letter Award for Tennis

40

brought on by spina bifida killed any aspirations I had of turning into an NCAA tennis player. I was coming out of a high school from which maybe thirty percent of the graduates went on to attend college, so I felt lucky to have any options—especially fortunate to have a tennis coach who also taught biology.

Coach Fred Wightman, also my biology teacher, was one of the most important people in my life, thanks in part to my brothers, who preceded me at Central. When we got to Tulsa, An and Ross were high school seniors and sophomores, respectively. Their tennis skills began to peak when they arrived at Central, which had never been a prominent presence on the local tennis scene. So, Coach Wightman took a liking to them right away. They both ended up making All-City and helping him gain recognition for the first time. Frank was the one who helped get my brothers the attention of the coach at his alma mater, Baker College. My sister went there, too, thanks to Coach Wightman's pipeline. When I got to Central, Coach Wightman was waiting. He taught me biology, coached me in tennis, and talked me into joining his Swim Team. I made All-City in that sport, too. Coach Wightman got me an offer from Baker, too, but I had different plans.

The coolest thing Coach Wightman did for me and my siblings was to introduce us to Frank Ward, Tulsa's Mr. Tennis. Frank Ward was executive director of the Tulsa Area Tennis Association for over half a century. In those days, Coach Ward ran the local USTA tournaments in the Tulsa area and was also in charge of popular summer camps. Coach Wightman was so determined to put Central on the tennis map that he paid for my brothers and me to compete in Ward's tournaments. We did well enough to garner an introduction to the legendary coach. Between the two of them, neither I, my sister, nor my brothers had to pay to play in the local USTA tournaments again. We even got to do a two-week summer camp. It was as close to a fancy academy as I ever got as a player, and it was heaven. For two weeks, they drilled us and taught us how to refine our skills—taught us strategy. When Frank eventually retired, I signed a check for $5,000 to contribute towards his retirement, thanking him for all he had done for our family.

I stayed in contact with Coach Wightman for life, too. I had to. I probably failed every test in his class and still earned a B! You could say my backhand showed enough potential to put just the right curve on my grade-point average. Seriously, Coach Wightman was a fantastic gentleman. He was a graduate of Central High School himself. Then, in 1964, he went to Baker to play tennis and earn a BS in biology, which he would later teach. He and his wife, Randi, were married for fifty years before he tragically died in 2021. I was lucky enough to have lunch with Coach Wightman again before he passed away. By then, he was retired and told me about his travels to Bhutan, Easter Island, Madagascar, Antarctica, and other fabulous destinations. Coach Wightman truly was an educator and mentor to me and my family.

Graduating from high school with English not yet a second language required plenty of extra credit work to get into college. I still think in Vietnamese to this day. My English improved after I received my diploma, but it was still below the average of college students. So, I used knowledge gained from growing up in a family full of alphas. I understood the dynamics of value and leverage, as well as how to negotiate them.

That was at school, but I learned equally important business skills working restaurant jobs as a teenager. I couldn't have believed in my wildest dreams that I was in career training at fourteen, but I was. Thanks to a classic Italian restaurant in Tulsa, I doubled up on my education in high school. I didn't realize it was essential to my chance of getting through college, but I see it clearly now. And just like any gambling hot streak, there was just enough luck.

Ban's high school graduation - 1980

Sports, such as swimming and tennis, provided me with a platform to showcase my skills and demonstrate value. They carried me through those years, and although I had a lot of fun playing tennis and competing on the swim team, neither of those activities brought me any financial gain. With my older brothers off playing tennis at Baker, the only thing for me to do was give working a swing. But before I could fill out an application, my dad found me a job that was a lot of fun and helped lay the foundation for a life working in hospitality. I started working at restaurants in high school to earn money, but I also received the education I needed there, just as much as the one that earned me a diploma to attend college.

My dad left Earl Stehle's gas station when he found a better job. After the stress and pressure of military life, my dad found peace of mind and a long and fruitful career repairing time clocks. I was fourteen when he returned from fixing one at Peppe's Italian Villa Capri. He asked the office lady if they had work for a 14-year-old boy. She answered, "Yeah, we got an opening for a busboy."

The next day, I dropped by to complete an application and started that weekend. I worked for peanuts, but I kept busing tables at Peppe's Italian Villa Capri, located at 6125 S. Sheridan Road, until I graduated because it paid off in more than just money. A gentleman named Joseph Shelfo and his wife, Marlene, owned Peppe's. Joseph was a veteran operator from Cleveland, Ohio, by way of California. There was a second location downtown in the Ambassador Hotel. Both were extremely popular. Italian restaurants were all the rage in those days, and the style was semi-formal. Servers wore ruffled shirts under red jackets, and the restaurant served cocktails even though serving liquor at a restaurant was more complicated in those days. Peppe's was from a completely different era. Spaghetti and meatballs drove a 72-item menu, and on weekends, the owner walked through the dining room playing accordion while a twelve-year-old kid accompanied on the piano. We handled everything from formal seated dinners to walk-ins on the same night with no problem.

Working at Peppe's taught me much about the hospitality industry but didn't necessarily prepare me to spread Jimmy's Egg franchises around the country. What I learned was human resources, customer service, and preparation. I started at Peppe's as a busboy and worked my way up to waiter by graduation. As a waiter, I learned to work effectively, support my colleagues, and prioritize customer service. I learned how hard it is to do one without the other. Teamwork makes the dream work, right? Sure, Peppe's was my first exposure to restaurant operations and the hospitality industry, but the most important, or at least memorable, lesson I learned was how to tie a cherry stem into a knot using only my tongue.

My tutor's name was Vicky. She was in her late twenties or early thirties and ran the bar at Peppe's. She looked exactly like the country & western singer Crystal Gayle: those big blue eyes and long, dark hair. Trust me, it's a Seventies thing – if you know, you know. Anyone my age and as inexperienced with the opposite sex was bound to fall at once under her spell. She drew plenty of customers to the cocktail bar at Peppe's, which you would've had to have a membership to get a drink back then. Thank goodness it was the waning days of liquor-by-the-drink (or wink!), but I digress. Vicky was a co-star of a cast of characters who groomed me for the career ahead. I saw my dedication as a busboy pay off more than once. I watched Mr. Shelfo go to town on a new waiter who tried to shortchange me one night. Peppe had never seen me lose my temper, so he had my back when he saw me rear back to throw the handful of change this guy had shared with me in tips. That guy did not last long.

He was nothing compared to Mr. Shelfo's stepdaughter. After he brought her into the restaurant to work, he started coming up to me, "You gotta go out with my stepdaughter." I knew nothing about girls then; this girl was ready to teach me. I was afraid she would corner me in the walk-in and make a man of me, whether I wanted her to or not! I received my first kiss while working at Peppe's, but I never had a girlfriend in high school. I didn't have a college girlfriend either, but I did plenty of running around looking for one. Peppe's helped me afford a used, four-door Toyota Celica right after my sixteenth birthday. It might not have helped me find a girlfriend, but it sure helped me look for one.

It also came in handy with Vicky, the Crystal Gayle lookalike. Once I had a car, she would sometimes call me and ask for a ride to work. Carpooling deepened my crush on her, and she knew it. She flirted with me all the time, pinched my butt sometimes when I walked by and treated me like I was closer to twenty-seven than sixteen or seventeen. She only teased me, but even at sixteen, I could see Vicky had a crush on someone else. Her crush was on the same person everyone at Peppe's had a crush on—a big, barrel-chested Iranian guy named Johnny. He was an absolute stud, right? Everyone could see it and knew it. Not just good looks, but charisma, too. All the staff wanted to work during Johnny's shifts, and every customer wanted to eat in his section. Mr. Shelfo sent every big party to Johnny, who was generous to the whole staff. He knew how to get people to cooperate with him, whether they were customers or colleagues. He also had amazing long hair, very fashionable at the time, plus a long beard to complete his legendary status. Even a dumb teenager like me could see that Johnny and Vicky were hot for each other. After Vicky got divorced, it was crystal clear. I was a witness to it. One day, I drove over to pick up Vicky for work, and she didn't hear me honking. So, I went to the door to knock on it, but it was open. I slowly peeked my head inside and *theeerrrreeeeeee'sssssssssssssss Johnny*!

I guess she forgot to call to tell me she'd already found a ride that day, but it didn't stop her from giving me that lesson of a lifetime. Learning to knot up cherry stems in my mouth was a lesson that helped as much as arithmetic in college. It happened one night after closing. Vicky tells me she's going to teach me about girls.

"You need to learn how to tie a knot out of a cherry stem using only your tongue," she said. "You do that, and the older girls will love you."

Then Vicky plucked a cherry by the stem from a jar of cocktail cherries, sat on the bar, and popped it in her mouth. Less than thirty seconds later, she showed me the stem lying on her tongue, neatly tied in a knot. I asked her to do it a few times so I could learn how to do it. I watched her as intently as I had watched my brothers play tennis years before and learned even faster. I guess Vickey was a better teacher than either of them. After showing me a few times, Vicky slid the jar of cherries my way and said, "Practice."

When you're sixteen and a lady who looks like Crystal Gayle tells you to do something, you do it. Half a jar of cherries later, I figured it out. If you give me a cherry stem, I can still tie it in a knot using only my tongue. It's my only superpower. It might not have been essential to college success, but it didn't hurt.

What did hurt, at least a little, was the path to college. My English verbal skills were functional by the time I was eighteen, but the struggle was real when it came to writing in English. Learning to tongue-tie a cherry in a knot came easier to me than avoiding sentence fragments and misspellings. Because my English writing skills were still remedial, my ACT score was only 12. That was my first real introduction to something I rely on today: Orange Power (aka Oklahoma State University)!

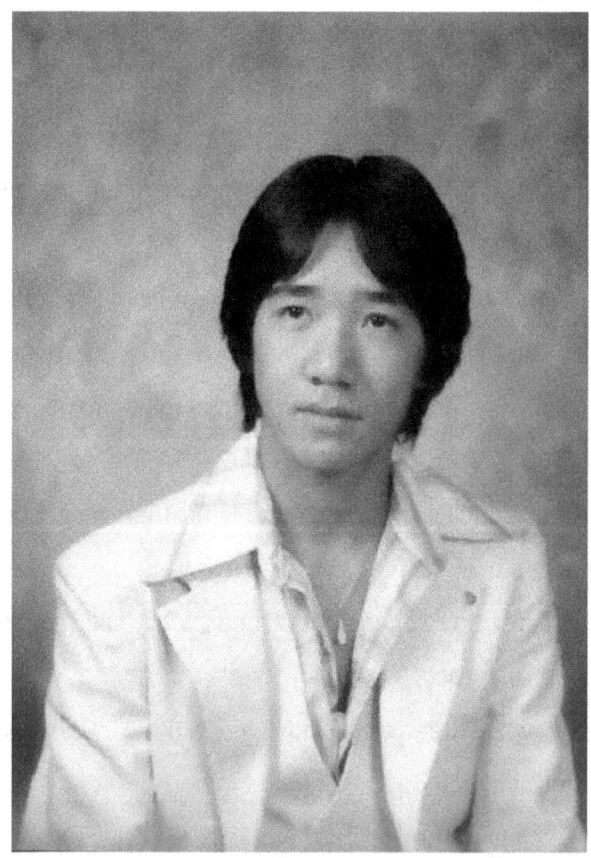

Ban's senior photo

Four

Classroom Daze, Swinging Nights

Good luck has followed me in so many ways, but when it comes to college, I found it in Stillwater. Oklahoma State University's entrance standards in 1980 were extremely liberal. Lucky for me, the only university in the state that would take me, and my 12 ACT score, was OSU. In retrospect, I can't imagine where I would be today if my path had not run through Stillwater. I had no idea it was home to one of the best schools in the country for aspiring restaurateurs, nor did I realize that a career in hospitality lay ahead of me. All I knew was that even a guy who only scored twelve on the ACT could become a "poke" (cowpoke) as long as you were in the seventieth percentile of your high school graduating class. Even my struggles with English class didn't stop me from graduating in the top twenty-fifth percentile at Tulsa Central High School.

Confidence was the key to success in college, and I was brimming with it when I arrived in Stillwater in the fall of 1980. It was confidence built on finding a way into the twenty-fifth percentile despite language challenges, swatting away bullies, and building enough athletic prowess to make the local newspapers. Confidence was founded on my father's insistence that his kids bring an alpha approach into the world. This confidence, cobbled together over four years slinging pasta to pay for a car while learning to socialize with women willing to teach me to train my tongue for future use, also came from swimming pools and tennis courts, where my work ethic was honed. In sports, I could see the fruits of my labor gain notice and appreciation. Nothing builds confidence faster than people recognizing your value. College would provide even more non-traditional education. It helped me grow in many ways. Ways that were more fun than good. Even though Peppe's had a full cocktail bar, I learned to drink in Stillwater! That's right, Stillwater was a whole experience. I never drank or partied in high school, but Peppe's provided a good enough sneak peek to make me want to jump feet first as soon as I got to OSU. But not before a spell of caution.

In my freshman year in Stillwater, I excelled. I went to class and studied in my dorm room as a normal student would and should do. OSU was a hell of a lot bigger than Tulsa Central and so much nicer. It was intimidating at first. So were the classes. Although much of it was review from high school, I was still significantly behind in reading and writing. It did help me catch up, but just when I started to feel comfortable, a class like Speech came along. A class where you first write a speech in English and then you've got to read it in front of the class!?! My worst nightmare. I remember how scared I was about my first assignment in Speech class. This was a required class for graduation. No dropping. I was shaking through the whole thing.

I was so scared I would flunk that I went to talk to the teacher. She told me to pick a subject I was confident talking about, something I could speak about, song and verse. I would find my confidence. So, I brought two tennis rackets to class and made a speech about tennis. She helped me transfer some of the confidence I'd earned playing tennis to my fear of speaking in front of people. I still remember how frightened I was of that class and how my teacher helped me, which is a testament to her wisdom. My experience with OSU faculty was a series of experiences like that, even after a dramatic sophomore swoon.

In my sophomore year, what started as a pretty good grade-point average took a dramatic nosedive. That happened not long after I discovered Eskimo Joe's on Monday nights. Stan Clark's iconic bar and restaurant was mostly a watering hole back in those days, but the cheese fries were hot, the beer was cold, and it was the place everyone in Stillwater, Cowboy or not, went on Monday nights. The freedom was exhilarating. Out on my own, I could experiment. I felt like I could spread my wings away from my parents' rules, even if it were to do something as mundane as guzzle cheap 3.2-beer. Starting on Monday nights, I learned how to do just that and got drunk for the very first time. I count Eskimo Joe's founder and owner, Stan Clark, among my best friends today. His story is almost as miraculous as mine. Eskimo Joe's on Mondays grew into two-stepping at Tumbleweeds and watered-down beer and whiskey at Cimarron Ballroom on the weekends.

The most memorable tradition for anybody attending OSU in the early 1980s was Wednesday nights at Willie's Saloon. The *Urban Cowboy* phase that the US was tired of by 1982 was alive and well in Stillwater, Oklahoma. The local talent was incredible. Singers and songwriters from all over Oklahoma were drawn to The Strip where Willie's was. On one of those Wednesdays, I first saw a skinny kid from Yukon named Garth Brooks at Willie's. He sang a lot of covers at first. Not even country songs, necessarily. However, he began performing some of his original material before leaving for Nashville. I was singing along to "I Got Friends in Low Places" before it was ever recorded! At least, that's how I remember it through the shots and watered-down beer. And do you know what? Everybody needs to go through a period like that. I told my kids the same thing. You need to go through it. You will experience it to learn your limits and prepare yourself for what lies ahead in the real world. So, of course, during the first two years, I partied hard. It's true. But you know, I'm proud to say I had a really fun time barely making it. And sure, it cost me a grade-point average: no honor roll or Dean's List for me. Guess what? That doesn't stop various Deans at OSU from calling me regularly these days!

To get to Garth and Willie's, I skipped over a significant milestone that occurred early during my sophomore year. I joined the Lambda Chi Alpha fraternity and moved into its house, where I served as the kitchen manager. All I knew about Lambda Chi Alpha was that my dorm neighbor, Kevin Clark, was attending one of their parties and had invited me to come along. I just followed him to the party, and the next thing I knew, Kevin and I were roommates in a fraternity house. Kevin and I remain friends to this day, but I also made many good friends during that time. You learn a lot from living with a group of eighty guys, especially if you're as shy as I was. But you learn to negotiate when you live with eighty guys in a fraternity house.

Lambda Chi Alpha - 1982

That year was a lot of fun, but I ended up on academic probation with the business school in the second semester. My GPA for that semester? One. It was not quite *Animal House* territory, but I was on my way. It was a lot of fun until I received the probation letter from the Dean. It said I would be out if I didn't improve my grades. One way or another. That summer was pivotal. My first impulse was to reach for my Plan B and join the military. My brother Ross did it, and it served him well. So, I decided to join the Marines. Just like Bill Murray in *Stripes* – what a great place to start! I really did try to enlist. But I did not pass the physical. The same spina bifida that hindered me since I was a young man and ended up curtailing my tennis career kept me out of the Marines. That's when I had to straighten up. That's when I realized, "Boy, you better study and try harder if you want to get a job after school." Up until that point, my Plan B was simple: "Hey, just have fun, make it through, and if anything goes wrong, join the military. Follow in your dad's footsteps; he was a career military man." With my only Plan B cooked, I had no choice but to bear down. I changed majors, too. I started at OSU as a Computer Science major before switching to Accounting. However, after receiving a D in my first accounting class, I shifted my focus to management information systems. That was just one of the suggestions the school made that ultimately helped me improve my situation. Henceforth, I did a better job of balancing my studies with my social life.

Ban in front of OSU Theta Pond

The other thing I did that summer was fine-tuning my backhand down the line into a weapon on the tennis courts. Although I didn't play for the Oklahoma State tennis team, I remained active in intramurals and amateur tennis, participating in various state and sectional tournaments.

Swinging and Slinging

Tennis remained a vital outlet for me throughout my college years. Throughout high school, my tennis game relied heavily on court coverage and defense. It was like playing against a wall. To beat me, I was going to make you hit winners. Somewhere along the way, I must've hit 10,000 hours of practicing the backhand while playing intramural tennis. All I know is that my backhand down the line became a weapon. Back then, if you wanted to compete in tournaments, you had to have an NTRP (National Tennis Rating Program) rating. Mine got up to 4.5, which made me a B-plus player at the intermediate or advanced level. Suddenly, my summer hobby of keeping in shape started earning me some serious hardware. The same shelves where my nunchucks hang bear the trophies I accumulated playing tennis for most of my life. I continued to play well into my thirties before pain related to the spina bifida turned me into my kids' coach.

The improvement of my tennis game followed the same trajectory as my confidence as I neared the end of my four-and-a-half years in Stillwater. I left with an MIS degree, and from the depths of that 1.0 semester came the 2.17 GPA I'm still proud of today. Look, I didn't stop having fun. The truth is, I probably had more fun once I got my studies straightened out. You carry a lot of stress when you are on the verge of flunking out of school. Maybe that was my first time learning to manage stress. All I know is that once I got on a better academic path, I could relax and have a good time. Many people might not boast about a 2.17 GPA, but that's a long way to climb from where I started. Besides that, it was exhausting becoming what I am pretty sure was the school's first Vietnamese frat boy!

Just like in Tulsa, I was marginalized because of my race, but I didn't have to use my nunchucks on anybody. My fraternity brothers didn't call me Bruce Lee, but they did call me Hop Sing. Younger folks might not understand the reference, but Hop Sing was a Chinese character on the television show *Bonanza.* Set in the Old West, *Bonanza* depicted a widower and his three grown sons living on the range. Without a matriarch to cook and clean, the Cartwright family employed Hop Sing for those domestic duties. It didn't help that I was the kitchen manager. Even though my brothers' joking was good-hearted, it did lead to a few fights. But overall, the fraternity experience was more than I could've asked for. It helped my confidence even more. OSU was a wonderful experience and a wonderful place to grow up. College was a balance of good times and education, and once again, education didn't always come from a classroom. Many of the most important lessons I learned in college didn't come from a textbook or lecture. Thanks to those three years of my life in the Lambda Chi house, I can now converse with anyone. Maybe nothing prepared me to operate restaurants as much as Lambda Chi Alpha. Don't forget, I had plenty of practice in assimilation before I arrived in Stillwater. That practice began abruptly a week before Saigon fell. Going to college and joining a frat was part of that process. But the fraternity, in particular, helped shape my people skills. I'm unsure if learning to get along can be a superpower, but this might be evidence, considering that this graduate with a 2.17 GPA is now on the advisory board for Oklahoma State's School of Hospitality and Tourism Management and the Board at the Business School. I was even invited to serve as CEO for a day by OSU's

All Vietnamese Midwest region (1985)

Dean of the College of Business. Being in a frat was the prime place to learn that it's not always what you know but who you know. Hard work shouldn't be reserved for your grade point average. Save plenty of that work ethic for your social life and social experiences. Human resources are ultimately the most valuable resource we can have in life. The lifelong relationships I made in Stillwater remain some of the most valuable relationships I've ever had, and they continue to pay dividends.

Leaving OSU with that MIS degree in the fall of 1984, I felt I could tackle anything. I even got a good job in the computer industry pretty quickly. Until that point in my life, the only thing it felt like I'd consistently swung and missed at was love. That was about to change. In fact, a lot was about to change—not only in my love life but also in my career trajectory.

Five

Heart Strings and Baby Swings

During a period of remarkable change, incredible opportunity, and a steady diet of learning, I took my first real swing at love. I hate to brag, but that first swing was a grand slam. My wife, Yen, and I have been married for almost forty years, and together, we have raised three beautiful children into adulthood. Yen is not only a fantastic wife and mother but also an incredible business partner. As a bonus, Yen is still the most beautiful woman in any room and a reminder of the ridiculous trifecta I hit when it comes to family.

The family I was born into prepared me to survive and thrive. The family I started with Yen continues to fill my heart with joy and inspires me to build on the Jimmy's Egg legacy. Finally, the family I wed into proved to be as remarkable as the one that raised me. It is indeed a rare family trifecta. The kind that laid a foundation that set us up for success at home and in business... a foundation strong enough to sustain a chain of restaurants and open the door to a legacy the entire family can grow with each new generation. But it all started because my little sister was further down the road in her love life than I was in 1984.

That was my last year at Oklahoma State. Until then, I chased my share of girls, and by my last semester, I was finally dating someone fairly steady. Meanwhile, my youngest sister, Trang, had a wedding on the calendar that fall. The girl I dated at the time happened to be one of her bridesmaids. As it turned out, Trang's wedding inspired me to take a swing at love—only it wasn't with the bridesmaid I was dating! I attended all the wedding party functions with this bridesmaid, but there was this gorgeous girl who came with the best man. She almost made my heart stop. She was one of my sister's roommates at Central State University in Edmond, Oklahoma, a bedroom community north of Oklahoma City. Throughout the celebration, several people, including my little sister, introduced me to a girl named Yen Khanh. A flirtation began, and she eventually told me she wasn't dating the best man. She said she had only come with him to attend the wedding parties.

After the festivities, I returned to Stillwater to finish my degree. I buckled down and concentrated on crossing all my T's and dotting all my I's, so when December came, I did two things: collected my MIS degree and broke it off with the bridesmaid I'd been dating at the wedding. Next, I went west looking for Yen in Oklahoma City. I went to stay with Trang for a little while, but Yen was nowhere to be found. She was in California visiting a friend. So, of course, when Yen returned to Oklahoma, my little sister immediately called her old roommate to say, "Guess what? My older brother was here looking for you!"

60

Swinging and Slinging

I guess the rest is history, but if you ask Trang, she'll tell you she sold me to my wife for $449. Yen, who kept the books at Jimmy's Egg for years, started when she was young. When she and my sister were roommates, Yen kept track of the money for utility bills and rent. Trang was short of money towards the end and told Yen, "Tell you what, I've got a brother I think you're gonna like. Let's call the $449 credit, and I'll put my brother up as collateral." My sister never paid Yen, and they still talk about how I got put on layaway.

Yen and I dated for almost two and a half years. It started long-distance. Right out of OSU, I got a job with my degree near Tulsa while Yen finished up at Central State. About two years into my brand-new career in the tech industry, it all came crashing down.

When I entered college in 1980, I had computers on my mind. There was a good reason for that. During the late 1970s and early 1980s,

Ban and Yen dating

computer systems began to replace antiquated filing systems and infiltrated businesses and homes for the first time. It seemed the correct field for me to explore as a young man. I chose computers because I saw potential going forward, but what I didn't factor into my calculations was how poor my vision is! Vision has never been a strength. I'm not exactly blind, but a color-blind father raised me! I'm not so much the big-picture guy as the guy who shows up to get things done. Luckily, I was on a collision course with one of the greatest visionaries Vietnam has ever produced.

As I mentioned, immediately after graduating from OSU, I was able to secure a job in the computer field. It made me feel like a real big shot when my MIS degree landed me a job in Sand Springs, just outside Tulsa, called Southwest Tube Manufacturing. I was creating systems for them, but even before my two years were up, I knew this wasn't the job for me. My exit from the tech industry was precipitated by economic conditions that led to the Black Monday crash of October 19, 1987. In Oklahoma, fluctuating oil prices made the local economy tissue soft. Between the two, the job market tanked. It was time to make a change.

Yen and I had dated long enough that her family had embraced me by then. When I arrived in town, her parents allowed me to stay in an extra room they had in their house. Once the computer thing went by the wayside, her family always had a room for me. We built a great rapport. Since I no longer had a job in Tulsa, our long-distance relationship came to an end. Yen's family was gracious enough to let me stay in the spare room. Her parents knew the only place I had to stay in Oklahoma City was with Trang and her new husband in a tiny apartment. Of course, they also knew I was fresh out of a job and didn't have the money to afford a place yet. They were also anxious for Yen and me to get married, which we did on December 20, 1986.

In early 1987, the economy was struggling nationwide, particularly so in Oklahoma. Oil was down to eight dollars a barrel back then—it might have even hit six dollars a barrel a couple of years before.

Ban and Yen on their wedding day

Ban and Yen in the early years

Regardless, the job market was so bad that I spent about nine months searching for a solution. As fate would have it, the solution was right under the roof we shared with Yen's family.

Luckily, the home was large enough to take on growth. Our first son, James, was born on July 11, 1987. So, of course, when he got older, he said, "Dad, that's only seven months." You can't get anything past that kid. Math is second nature, thanks to his Vietnamese roots! Number two, Khoi, arrived in December 1989. About four years after Khoi arrived, we endured a miscarriage. It was devastating and painful, but four years later,

Pauline was born. When Yen was pregnant with Pauline, I knew she would be a girl.

I was *so* sure I would've almost bet my life on it. Our little girl arrived in November 1997. Eleven years after we got started, our family was complete with two boys and a spoiled baby girl. They're all well-adjusted adults now.

My Pauline has matured into an intelligent young woman and the COO of Jimmy's Egg, but she's still pretty spoiled today! After the COVID-19 pandemic, Pauline came home from school on the East Coast and introduced us to her boyfriend. He was in a similar position to the one I found myself in back in 1986. Fortunately, we live in a home with plenty of room, so we took him in while he looked for work. Yen and I talked later about how that had been a full-circle moment. Without the grace of my in-laws, who knows what direction our lives would have taken?

Of course, my in-laws, Loc Van Le and Kim Vue Le, weren't ordinary in any way. That began with their grace but also encompassed a myriad of good qualities, including vision and determination. We lost Loc and Kim to complications from COVID-19 in December 2020. They were taken far too soon, but the outsized life they shared built a legacy that will never be forgotten. I've told people for years what a tycoon Mr. Loc Le was back in Vietnam. Donald Trump would've been jealous of what Loc accomplished before age thirty. He made his first million by the time he was in his early twenties. A true wheeler-dealer. When he was forced to flee the country, he left behind six businesses, including a trucking line, housing developments, a canned food company, and a lumber yard. In 1975, he was the Chief of Customs in Da Nang, and the US Department of

Ban and Yen with their children (James, Khoi, and Pauline)

Defense owed him more than $800,000 for work he had done for the US military. When he left Vietnam, Loc had no possessions or wealth. It took all he had left to buy a small commercial fishing boat in April 1975. He crammed about thirty people, including his family and friends, aboard the boat and set off into open water. They got as far as a freighter, where they were given water and invited to move on, but Loc clung to the freighter's anchor line and swore that if the freighter didn't take them on board, he and his family would die. The captain finally relented, and Loc burned the fishing boat he had spent the rest of his wealth on before they sailed away. Loc and Kim were true boat people. They spent about a month at sea before being taken in as refugees at Camp Pendleton in California. Once on dry land, the family took advantage of any available sponsorship opportunities, which led them to Hawaii, Nebraska, and Texas. An aunt and uncle who were members of Our Lady's Cathedral offered sponsorship in Oklahoma City to Loc and Kim, finally landing them in Oklahoma City by 1978.

The great Loc Van Le was no stranger to showing grace under pressure. He was born in 1945 to a wealthy family in Da Nang. Even though he'd only known wealth and learned to compound it at a young age, he had no trouble adapting to poverty. Penniless, homeless, and vaguely familiar with the language of his new home country, he and my mother-in-law, Kim, relished the challenge of entering this country and starting anew. Loc used to say he enjoyed a fifty-cent taco if that was all he could afford because he was a fighter and a survivor. Loc's most excellent skill was making the best of what was available instead of just dreaming about it.

Finding Oklahoma City must have been a dream come true for Loc and Kim three years after the fall of Saigon. They gravitated toward the growing Vietnamese community in what is now known as the Asian District. There, they found restaurants, markets, and specialty shops catering to the influx of Vietnamese immigrants. Loc and Kim went straight to work. She opened Hi-Fashion Wigs on North May Avenue, and Loc used his knowledge of freight and distribution to find a job with the Santa Fe Railroad Company. They also worked hard to learn English, which they believed would help their chances of building a business. They were right; Kim had gotten into the habit of opening the wig shop and then running down to grab breakfast at the little diner on 16th May, owned by Jim Newman. That's where she first heard that the place, Jimmy's Egg, might be for sale. Kim was the one who told Loc how good Jimmy's Egg was, but it was always closed by the time he got off work at the railroad. Once he finally had breakfast there, Loc agreed with my mother-in-law's assessment. Had he never made it over for eggs and hashbrowns, Jimmy's Egg was likely bound to become another forgotten breakfast joint people might struggle to remember. With Loc's business acumen, he and Kim probably would have made their fortune selling wigs. Thank God Kim saw that little diner shortly after Loc lost his thumb working on the railroad. The injury was the last straw for a job that would never help Loc rebuild his fortune.

Shortly after Loc's fateful breakfast at Jimmy's Egg, he and Kim contacted Newman about a price. My role didn't materialize for another seven years, but it was full steam ahead once Yen and I climbed aboard the Jimmy's Egg train. We went from a couple to a family of five in eleven years. And Jimmy's Egg? It swung wide open and went nationwide, which is why sharing my family story can go no further without sharing the story of our family business.

Six

Jimmy's Egg Swings into Action

A few years ago, the *Made In Oklahoma* exhibit chose Jimmy's Egg to be part of at the Oklahoma History Center. When I think back on that, it still gives me chills. Mostly, the "made in Oklahoma" part. I'm so proud of how our family has affected the Oklahoma story, not just our harrowing escape from political and social chaos but also the struggle to survive and assimilate that followed. So many cultures came to Oklahoma as refugees or due to forced migration; ours was hardly unique. That's what I love about it. Our family arrived at this melting pot and wrote another chapter in the Oklahoma story, primarily due to how we conducted our business.

The secret of our success at Jimmy's Egg is pretty simple: family. We've had the same menu for nearly forty years, but we provide a family environment. Sure, it's a family-friendly environment for our customers, but Jimmy's Egg is a family environment long before we open and leave for the day. It has been nearly four decades since my father-in-law, Loc Le, bought it. Our processes are all overseen by the family. I do a lot myself, and I do it from the comfort of my home. I don't lease a fancy office when I have a pretty fancy one in my house. And if I'm not working from home, I work out of my car. My wife, Yen, contributes daily, even though she's handed off much of the bookkeeping to my son, James, a certified public accountant. We all wear many hats. Cooks and the wait staff come straight to me or Yen with problems. There's no regional manager, kitchen manager, assistant manager, or bureaucracy.

There are a lot of ways to succeed in the restaurant industry. History has proven this. Our way is family-style. We don't serve meals family-style, but we are a chain of family-owned restaurants that strive to create a family atmosphere for our customers. Opening stores around Oklahoma and other parts of the country, I've seen it firsthand. For instance, the Degraffenreid family has found tremendous success with BoomARang Diners. They've got their niche, targeting small towns and leaving a small footprint. It works for them; they have over fifty stores to prove it. In the last few years, they've gravitated toward bigger markets. They've operated in Bethany and took over a Johnnie's Express in Edmond to gradually grow their footprint. It's a different approach, but you can't argue with success.

Our success at Jimmy's Egg stretches to an extended family. We own twenty-four of the seventy Jimmy's Egg locations. They are in eleven states, including Missouri, Kansas, Nebraska, Arkansas, Texas, Alabama, and New York. Ownership of our twenty-four stores is spread among more than a dozen family members. It's impossible to offer anything but a family environment from a business so steeped in family. I experienced the family environment of Jimmy's Egg for the first time in the winter of 1985 at 1616 North May Avenue. That was the last free meal I ever got at Jimmy's Egg. Not long before Yen and I married, I went to work at 1616

North May Avenue and quickly got a pair of singed eyebrows as initiation. I had no intention of staying there, but the more I learned, the more attractive it became. In the beginning, Jimmy's Egg was just another in a long line of breakfast diners and counters that populated the streets of Oklahoma City. Jimmy Newman started Jimmy's Egg in 1978 in the Victoria Building on Classen Boulevard. The classic building still stands, and the space is now home to another great breakfast restaurant, Café Antigua. Newman moved to the location on 16th and North May about a year before selling the business. That's right, *selling* the business. There's some fake news rolling around out there that Jimmy's Egg was won in a poker game. Loc loved to gamble like any red-blooded Vietnamese, but he paid Jimmy Newman $40,000 in 1980 for the business. The only restaurant I know of that was won in a poker game is Cattlemen's Steakhouse in the 40s!

Loc's deal with Jimmy included keeping him around as a consultant for six months to teach Kim and him the business. Loc was unsure the deal would work, so he kept his job at the railroad for another six months. After about a month as a consultant, Jimmy Newman took the money and ran. So, guess what? Loc had to jump in and learn from scratch how to cook. No problem, he jumped right on it and cooked every day. He and Kim learned the business as they went and leaned heavily on their employees.

Success came rapidly. Business was good enough to get Loc off the railroad while he still had nine good digits. Not only was Jimmy's Egg doing better than ever, but by 1983, Hi-Fashion Wigs grew into three locations, including one in Amarillo, Texas. They eventually sold the wig shops and invested in a new restaurant. Kim and Loc opened 23 Corner on NW 23rd Street and Western Avenue. It was much bigger than Jimmy's Egg, with 115 seats. It had been home to Rhett's and O'Hair's before, but 23 Corner never found a sustainable audience. Loc refocused on Jimmy's Egg, but size constraints limited how much revenue it could generate.

When I arrived in 1985, Jimmy's Egg was ready to expand. I could not find a job there, but I did have experience from Peppe's Italian Villa Capri and managing the Lambda Chi kitchen in college. Finally, I approached Loc and told him I was tired of rejection letters. It seemed like I sent out resumes every week, and all I would get back were rejection letters, three or four per week. Loc, whom I called Pop, was gracious when I asked him for a job at Jimmy's Egg. I started helping in the kitchen, cooking and washing dishes—whatever was needed. That was how I lost my eyebrows, trying to ignite a pilot light I should have left to professionals. But I stuck to it, and maybe two or three months later, I told Pop he could stay home a little bit. On the weekends, all the kids came out to help, but in those days, he was working six to seven days a week at that one location. Loc handed me the reins little by little for almost a year before I proved myself to him. That opened the door to my first big chance in business.

Yen and I had only been married a month at the beginning of 1987. She was carrying our first child, but I had a baby of my own to bring into this world: Jimmy's Egg No. 2. I was the general contractor for the job. I hired a construction guy and other subcontractors, including electricians, plumbers, and other specialists. I was there when the inspectors arrived. We put up the drywall ourselves. I oversaw everything.

You know what? That store only cost me $29,000, all told. Today, opening a store like that for Jimmy's Egg would cost half a million dollars. Of course, we now install brand-new equipment and furniture for our new locations. Back then, our timing was right. In the wake of the Bust and the coming Black Monday, many restaurants went out of business. We went to auctions and paid ten cents on the dollar for used equipment. The same kind of deals were available for the furniture. Jimmy's Egg No. 2 was a mishmash of color and décor, but it didn't bother us.

We opened Jimmy's Egg No. 2 on March 15, 1987, on MacArthur Boulevard, just north of Northwest Expressway, in Oklahoma City. Yen was five months pregnant, working as a waitress, helping in the kitchen, and handling cash. I was even busier because my baby had already arrived, and my daily task list grew every day during that period. The reason? Business was a smash. Yen was too busy waiting tables for the next four months, and I was too busy cracking eggs to even look up. As she got closer to summer, Yen stayed home with Kim more. I remember getting home after two o'clock in early July to find Yen vacuuming when, all of a sudden, her water broke. And we were off to Baptist Hospital. About twelve hours later, we welcomed James into the world. What a day. We didn't have much time to stop and smell the roses in those days, but Baby James was a cause for celebration. We took a moment to appreciate life, but not for too long! Our newborn restaurant was only four months old and felt like it needed almost as much attention as James! More sometimes. Sleep came at a premium in those days. I was used to getting up at four each morning, which was helpful for some early morning feedings. Indeed, it was a fortunate time to be young.

Jimmy's Egg No. 2 was almost twice as big as our original, so I knew we would have to promote it more. That's when I took a page out of my father's playbook. I remembered how successfully my father promoted Earl Stehle's gas station by going to the local media and sharing our story. That gave me the idea of introducing myself to Jack Elliott and Ron Williams of the old *Jack and Ron Show* on KISS-FM radio. Jack asked me to come to the station and bring breakfast, and that was all it took. Jack and Ron had us back many times after that. Like Earl Stehle's gas station, the free publicity did wonders for business. Suddenly, Jimmy's Egg was the most popular place for breakfast in Oklahoma City.

Loc was thrilled with our success at Jimmy's Egg No. 2, and Kim was even more delighted to have a grandson to spoil. Loc was a visionary businessman, and his senses told him it was time to expand. Jimmy's Egg won awards for best breakfast, business was booming at both locations, and Pops put his visionary skills into overdrive. With me there to attack whatever he needed to get done, whether negotiating or subcontracting, we opened a third restaurant together, then a fourth, and finally a fifth. We attacked it together while Yen and Kim helped with the books and Baby James. Conditions were ideal for growing both a business and a family. Yen and I still lived with Loc and Kim when baby number two came along.

Khoi was born in December 1989, and by then, Loc and I were getting more efficient at opening up stores. We opened locations in Midwest City and The Village simultaneously when Khoi arrived. Meanwhile, Yen was more efficient at having babies. Unlike James, who took half a day to enter the world, Khoi popped out in forty-five minutes!

Surprised she didn't have twins to go along with the two stores we were opening! The new Village location was right across from Casady School. We didn't know the area, but we learned about the prestigious private school across the street. We didn't realize we would spend twenty-five years there and send all three kids to Casady. After paying tuition for three kids to go through Casady, I jokingly told the headmaster I should own a piece of the rock somewhere on campus!

By 1990, Jimmy's Egg was at five locations. Loc and I worked side by side with John Krittenbrink and Krittenbrink Construction to get there. They have built Jimmy's Egg locations for more than thirty years. What excellent partners John and his team have been over the past three decades.

Once the fifth store opened, I told Loc I needed a break. I was cooking, managing, and opening new stores from 4 a.m. to 4 p.m., six days a week, while my wife and two kids were at home. Luckily, after the fifth store, some banks started noticing Jimmy's Egg. They offered us a crazy line of credit, and we took it. This allowed us to stop leasing so much and start building. We had to reach into our pockets for the first five stores to fund the expansion. Finding the right used equipment and furniture didn't always align with our present cash flow. With the help of bank loans, an efficient process took shape. The first five stores took us between seven and eight years to build. With the help of banks, the number of units grew from six to fifteen in just five to six years.

Growing into a chain of seventy establishments taught us innumerable good and bad lessons. We've had more ups than downs. The most important thing I learned from Loc was how to treat people in a professional business setting. It goes back to that family-style approach I mentioned at the beginning of the chapter. To grow the business as quickly as we did, we had to invite all our staff and contractors into the family to do business, just like the Krittenbrinks and many others. Loc taught me to treat people in business like family, whether they are employees or salespeople. Loyalty is the key, showing that it is the only way to gain people's loyalty.

Loc sponsored a number of our Hispanic employees who arrived without documents. He created a program for them to gain sponsorship. I remember there were at least three or four from the beginning, and he repaid their loyalty. He helped them obtain their green card, and he assisted them in securing a good living at Jimmy's Egg. They ended up bringing their families, and we still have a lot of people working for me to this day who were sponsored by us for their citizenship. I've been truly blessed with lots of good employees. I treat my employees like my family. They make the difference, not me. I understand my employees have to be there, and so I try hard to get to know them as people. Hell, I've done all the jobs they're doing, so it gives us something to talk about. Not many CEOs can be best buddies with the dishwasher. That was a lesson Loc taught me, and I saw how it instilled respect for him. In my capacity, I talk to them and listen to what's going on in their lives. If I'm going to expect professional hospitality from them, the least I can do is treat them with genuine hospitality. It's just about paying that hospitality forward. How good I am doesn't matter; I'm nothing without my employees.

One of our big successes was finding partners for a buying program. I called some of the restaurateurs I hang out with and said, "Hey, let's see if we can combine our buying power." If we bought common products, why not buy in bulk and save each other some money? That worked out great for all of us. Partnerships like that breed trust, and you can bet they will grow on word of mouth in the business community.

I was too busy cooking, cleaning, or running the register the first couple of years to look around. Hey, I just built myself a job out of nothing, right? I remember the first year we were in business with Jimmy's Egg No. 2, Yen and I calculated that we would make maybe $20,000 in salary. Then, a few years later, we hit $69,000 with two stores. I remarked to my wife how amazing it was to reach that height after coming here with nothing. By the time we were having those conversations, my job had evolved. There is not much cooking, cleaning, or taking cash anymore. Sure, there were emergencies, but once you develop those hospitality muscles, you're fit for life to work in a restaurant. But by that time, I was talking with banks a lot more. Finding new locations became my new job, and it was fun. Loc loved negotiation. He loved to talk about contracts. He loved building things. He taught me everything he knew about contract negotiations, which helped me fall in love with the same thing. I love to negotiate and agree on a handshake. I love how the stroke of a pen on a contract can make things happen. Over the years, it has become a fun experience. Deals don't have to be about restaurants for them to be fun to me; they can be anything. Business is a whole lot like gambling in that way.

After five stores in seven years, I felt like I'd become a businessman: Find the location, then negotiate the land or a lease. That was fun because it's not the stuff you learn from a college classroom.

Businesses, like tennis and nunchucks, required a self-taught swing. Luckily, I've had plenty of experience. Sure, I had a big S for sucker on my forehead many times. Things you didn't see coming taught me to look more carefully the next time and the time after that. Downturn and failure—call it what you want—comes with the territory. Just like a fraternity has an initiation, so does business. Failure is a great teacher, but as a business professional, you've got to be an even better student. Draw as much as possible from each failure so you don't have to go through as many in the future. And remember, many of us in business had to work hard for every dollar we've earned. It fosters an appreciation that can't be found in any school. At my age, I see how that appreciation has evolved. Hard work isn't something you can inherit. It usually goes the other way. I warn my Boomer friends that they tend to spoil their kids, especially my white friends. Look, I spoiled my kids some, but you don't do them any favors if you spoil them all along the way. My kids had to work from a young age. They've worked for their achievements, not just some freebie stuff.

Part of the reason I emphasized work for my kids is that not everything I did worked. Remember Jimmy's Chicken Fry? Nor does anyone else. Loc used to say, "I've been through many challenges, and I didn't always make it. I do not always succeed, but I am not a guy to be whining about it because I make happiness in any condition God gives to me." He had proof on his side, and that said it all for me—no reason to cry about missteps. Take my initial attempts to build a franchising program. We created a subsidiary company, Jimmy's Egg Franchise Systems LLC, to actively franchise the restaurant in April 2008. Twenty franchise locations were operating then, and I thought we were ready to explode. We were, but my approach was a case study involving too many handshakes and inadequate vetting. One of the lessons you learn in business is that there are bad actors. Motives run the gamut for bad actors in business, but desperation is usually an ingredient. If you sense desperation in a potential partner, let that be a red flag. After a retreat, we were able to right the expansion ship. After a painful, expensive education, Jimmy's Egg was able to gather itself and grow the way we always wanted it to. Sometimes, the moments that sting the most are the price of doing business—the price of success. I'm not going to tell you all the pain was worth it, especially when trust was broken, but I can tell you my family and I are better for it.

Probably my biggest failure was Casablanca American Bistro, which was at 13801 Quail Point Drive in Oklahoma City. I had this great, big building not far from our Jimmy's Egg near Quail Springs Mall. I wanted to put a Cheesecake Factory in it. My family loved that place, and we didn't have one in Oklahoma City at the time. I called the Cheesecake Factory corporate office and informed them that I had a location and expressed my interest in becoming a franchisee, but they stated that the company wasn't interested in the Oklahoma City market at that time. So, I decided I would make my own. I changed up the theme to be like Rick's Place in the movie *Casablanca*. A big bar and an even bigger dining room, with a smoking room in between. Antonio Velasquez was my executive chef, and we created a spectacular dining room featuring frosted glass etched with tiger lilies, large, comfortable booths, and a state-of-the-art ventilation system for the smoking room. Steve Blair created the design, and Krittenbrink did the construction. A guy named Stephen Edwards executed the sophisticated interior. Our wait staff wore slick black shirts with the Casablanca monogram. Like the Cheesecake Factory, we had a vast menu, including Vietnamese cuisine. Less than a year after we opened, Cheesecake Factory announced they were coming to Oklahoma City, and not long after that, we said, "Here's looking at you, kid," to Casablanca.

It was another hard lesson in the life of a small business. We do what we can, but small businesses are often the ones that have to make the hardest choices. Large corporations can pass their higher costs down the line, but small businesses are at the end of the chain. I buy a million pounds of potatoes a year. The truckload coming from the state of Washington to our warehouse once cost about $3,000. When gasoline prices and driver wages jumped, the same truckload suddenly cost $8,000. It's the same thing with equipment. The water heater that cost $3,000 to install costs $9,000 to replace. Things like that can mean the difference between whether or not you profit for the month. Margins are especially tight in restaurants. No one expected eggs to be twelve dollars a dozen or orange juice to jump 210 percent in four years. Factors like that are why the hard choice is often closing. We've closed stores and restaurants over the years for sure, but we consider ourselves blessed at Jimmy's Egg.

Charity has always been a significant part of the family and the business. Aside from pitching in after tragedies and supporting various causes, Loc was inspired by his first visit back to Vietnam in 1997. He was heartbroken to see the poverty overtaking parts of Da Nang. He eventually created the Le Family Trust Fund to build churches and schools in Vietnam. We continue that good work today.

As for my children, they all play roles in the business but maintain options for the future. My son, James, is the CFO of Jimmy's Egg and is a CPA. He worked at prestigious firms before, but in 2019, he approached me with an idea for a new concept. Later that summer, we opened Riviere Modern Banh Mi in Oklahoma City's Midtown next to a Jimmy's Egg location. Two years later, the whole family worked there during the pandemic. Yen even brought the meatballs she makes at home to the restaurant, which became a big hit. That energized me enough to open a second Riviere location in Edmond in a building we already owned.

In 2021, we demolished our original Jimmy's Egg location at 1616 North May Avenue with plans to rebuild an updated building that would serve as a proper memorial to Loc and Kim Le. My son Khoi has the design ready whenever we get the appropriate permitting to begin construction. Unfortunately, after several years, we're still not quite ready to move on with construction, but I can assure you we will. When we are, he'll have to get clearance from his little sister, Pauline, the COO for Jimmy's Egg. She will enjoy bossing her big brother around on that project. After that, who knows, maybe she'll get her commercial real estate license.

Whatever they do, the legacy their grandparents founded and the legacy their parents, aunts, and uncles have helped blossom across the country will be a part of it. That fact alone makes it harder for me to even think about retirement. But it does help me think more about trips to Las Vegas to gamble and work on my new favorite swings: golf and grandfatherhood.

Seven

Dynasty Construction is in Full Swing

As my business career enters its final act, I've lost no enthusiasm for the day-to-day and new opportunities. Negotiations are still fun for me. I love putting a deal in place and tracking it, like a garden—plant the seeds, provide water, then let sunshine and time provide the rest while you sit back and watch it all unfold. Everybody is in business to make money, of course, but what's fun is when you have a difficult project that looks like it's going bad but starts making money. Suddenly, business is fun. For instance, I made this deal with Taco Mayo to share a property with Jimmy's Egg at Reno and Council in west Oklahoma City. We made a deal to go in together and share this lot, and they came up with many great ideas to make this thing work. We asked ourselves if this was a mistake for the first few years. Gradually, revenues came, and profits ballooned.

The project required some time because it was backed by extensive operational experience and had sufficient funding to allow it to mature. It all starts to make sense when I think about it for a minute, because there is evolution in any career. It began with hustling for immediate gratification. I started learning the basics of the hospitality industry when I was just fourteen years old, busing tables as fast as I could to earn enough money for a used Toyota Celica. Simple math: Peppe's Italian Villa Capri was a means to a worthy end—chasing girls. So, I hustled for the money and learned a few unexpected lessons. Pretty simple.

Work took on new meaning once I was married and had a kid on the way. So much more was on the line. I was still hustling, but learning on the job... to soak in what was and wasn't working was much more important. No time for twisting cherry stems into knots! I had a business plan to conceive while I was cracking eggs. While the job required quick actions and fast learning, I had to slow down mentally to keep things straight.

Once Loc and I went into a full-court press expansion, the challenges grew, but so did the potential prize of growing a family business into a chain. The pressures and responsibilities were tremendous, but the reward was richer than rich. Because our family had experienced first-hand the life-saving value of an opportunity like this, we dug in. The small business dynasty Loc built before he was thirty saved not only Loc's life but also the lives of his wife and children. It's easy to see now how it saved generations of families. I witnessed it and was responsible for building a broader dynasty on the foundation Jimmy's Egg created after Loc's passing.

At his side for three and a half decades, I watched Loc like a hawk. I saw how he could cherry-pick specific properties, and we were able to turn them into tiny goldmines all around the city in the early days. I watched as we built our business circle based on loyalty and how he brought partners in and either kept them close or weeded them out over time. I even watched as he got older and lost some of the edge that made him successful. I saw him lose just enough of that initial hunger to let a few bad actors linger in the circle longer than he would have once upon a time. When I think about it now, I recognize how that happened, and it has made me hypersensitive to the fact that the Jimmy's Egg dynasty will need a succession plan to grow and prosper for our family in the coming generations.

I've picked up a few lessons with almost forty years under my belt as a restaurateur, developer, and entrepreneur. For instance, Rusty Shaw, one of the founders of OnCue, is a friend of mine—a good enough friend to share a simple equation that saves me between $5,000 and $6,000 each time we open a new store. Rusty taught me how he determined site locations for OnCue in the early days. He told me to set up at the nearest corner to the potential location with a clicker and spend ten minutes counting the cars that drive past. If it's a two-way intersection, count the back and forth. Count the cars going in either direction if it's a four-way intersection. Count for ten minutes, then multiply that number by two hundred, and you have a pretty accurate read on what kind of traffic you can expect for the location. Of course, you don't just do it at one time. You've got to hit that corner at strategic times to make the most accurate count. It also depends on what hours are important for the business.

Another lesson I've learned is the importance of diversifying assets for long-term growth. Riviere Modern Banh Mi is an example. When James brought me the idea, I had my eye on a property in Midtown for a new Jimmy's Egg. I was tired of seeing all these new breakfast places opening downtown Oklahoma City without competing with a Jimmy's Egg! I found a great property in Midtown, but it was too big for a Jimmy's Egg all by itself. We decided to split the building between Jimmy's Egg and Riviere. James and his mom's recipes not only survived the pandemic, but here in 2025, we're getting ready to open a second location in Edmond, Oklahoma.

However, as we grow the family business, it will absolutely remain a family business. How could it be anything else when so much of its DNA is built on the principle? Jimmy's Egg begins with family, but as I mentioned in the previous chapter, we strive to create a family-like atmosphere among our employees and business partners. One thing I've learned for sure is you can't do it alone. Loc's teachings only hammered the point home. He was a master at building loyalty, and I still apply this principle in practice. Maybe the most important example was when I first met Jack Elliott from *The Jack and Ron Show*. I mentioned how important that connection was before, but I didn't mention that I met Jack during a family outing. James was competing in a tennis tournament in Kansas City, and Jack's daughter was playing in the same tournament on the girls' side. I recognized Jack and struck up a conversation. We talked, and then he introduced me to his wife, an advertising executive for KFOR, the local NBC affiliate. Jimmy's Egg starts doing a little advertising with KFOR, and not long after, Jimmy's Egg gets the invite to deliver breakfast in the morning to KISS-FM. Everyone benefited in some way, and the interaction was a turning point in the history of Jimmy's Egg. Our trajectory began to trend upward gradually. Jack and Ron got complimentary breakfast each time we opened a new Jimmy's Egg. As I was adding new places, Jack and

Ron helped me put them on the map. Our time with Jack and Ron led to The Sports Animal, where we did the Jimmy's Egg in Your Face segment each Monday with local sports-talk legend Jim Traber for a long time. Total momentum shift, all expanding our business family on loyalty.

The loyalty Jimmy's Egg was founded on was never more important than when the COVID-19 pandemic arrived. Not only did it rob us of more time with Kim and Loc, but it also put the entire restaurant industry through the wringer. Jimmy's Egg was no exception. The restaurant industry was complex enough before the global pandemic stopped the world in its tracks. I tell anybody who asks not to enter the restaurant industry today! If I had tried to do this thirty years ago with the kinds of margins we have today, I would have closed down long ago. We've been fortunate enough to build up some reserves, which have allowed us to absorb some of the ups and downs we've gone through since the pandemic. But I'm not sure I'd know where to begin if I had to start from scratch today. If that sounds like I've quit, don't get it twisted. They tell me retirement age is only a couple of years away, but it feels like there is too much to accomplish before I start thinking about that. Energized by my children's contributions to the family business thus far, I've loved watching them develop as adults, parents, and business professionals. Their growth, maturity, and support from so many family members have made it much easier for me to work on a new swing: golf.

When I learned to play tennis in Vietnam, golf was not on our radar. Even as I grew up and started watching it on TV, I wasn't interested in playing. I played tennis at a very high level right into my forties. Even at that age, the USTA ranked me number one in the Missouri Valley among 4.5-level players. For three years in a row, no one could beat me.

Nevertheless, spina bifida is no joke. It's a condition I was born with, and I will manage the rest of my life. Golf happens to be a lot easier on my balky spine than tennis. Even though I hadn't considered golf a "real sport" for much of my life, I took to it quickly. Golf and tennis go together like salt and pepper. The swings are different, but not too much, at least not with my swing. It's more of a tennis swing and very right-hand dominant. I discovered that if I hold my right hand at a little angle, the result is a golf swing that serves me nicely. All this was self-taught, just like tennis, nunchucks, and business. I quickly picked up the game and fell in love with it even faster. I used to make fun of golfers, but now I play competitively for the Vietnamese Golf Association and am on a quest to play the Top 100 golf courses in America, as ranked by *Golf Magazine*. I'm currently right around fifty. The big one, of course, is Augusta National. Back when we still had about fifty stores, I ran into some bigwigs from Coca-Cola, and we talked about Augusta National because they're big sponsors of The Masters. I asked them about getting me on the course, and they told me I need to have eighty stores before we can talk. We're getting pretty close!

In the meantime, I've played most of the Top 50, including No. 6 Pebble. Beach, No. 22 Whistling Straits, No. 34 Southern Hills, No. 37 Butler National, No. 45 TPC Sawgrass, No. 99 Blackwolf Run (river), No. 40 Karsten Creek, No. 46 Cog Hill, No. 49 Cascata, No. 59 Black Mesa, No. 71 PGA West, No. 88 Ko'olau, No. 94 Doral, No. 95 Blackwolf Run (Meadow Valley), No. 80 World Woods, No. 91 TPC Louisiana, No. 85 Wolf Creek,

No. 100 Reflection Bay, No. 65 Firestone, No. 28 Prairie Dunes, No. 52 Eastlake Red Stone, No. 10 Pinehurst #2, No. 43 Bethpage Black, No. 3 Pacific Dunes, No. 6 Bandon Dunes, No. 12 Old Macdonald, No. 16 Bandon Trails, No. 48 Spyglass, No. 70 Olympia Fields, No. 69 Flint Hills National, No. 99 Streamsong Red, No. 24 Pelican Hill, No. 11 Sandhills, No.17 Muirfield Village, No. 37 Rich Harvest Farm, No. 58 Medinah #3, No. 84 Quintero, No. 71 Torrey Pines, and No. 21 Chamber Bay.

I'm just a guy trying to break eighty. So, any golf course where I break eighty becomes my new favorite. I played well at Spyglass but wasn't so great at Pebble Beach. So, I think Spyglass is better than Pebble Beach. Whistling Straits and East Lake were a lot of fun, too, and Sawgrass really stood out. I recently completed another bucket list by playing the top 10 golf courses in Las Vegas when I visited Shadow Creek and Southern Highlands. Internationally, I've played a lot in Mexico and Vietnam for VGA competitions, but nowhere in Europe. I would love to play in Scotland because it's the birthplace of golf.

I'm just as competitive at golf as tennis, but I recognize golf has value beyond taking a few bucks out of your buddy's wallet. Golf has a social aspect that's invaluable for business. Cashing in my tennis swing for a golf swing was destiny the minute my back hurt. Or maybe it was destiny the instant I got off the plane from the Philippines and set foot in Fort Chaffee, Arkansas. Perhaps switching from tennis to golf is part of the process of transitioning from youth to maturity. Adapting to the world around you is inevitable at home or in business. I learned that lesson when Saigon fell fifty years ago.

Swinging and Slinging

My family and my wife's family understood that if their kids were going to succeed in this country, they would have to learn how to live like Americans. That was one of the reasons Loc and Kim bought an American restaurant, especially an American breakfast diner. Serving eggs, pancakes, biscuits, and gravy ingrained us within the broader community. So many of my Vietnamese counterparts and neighbors have brought Vietnamese culture to Oklahoma. In Oklahoma City, the Asian District is one of the city's most flourishing entertainment and business districts. I'm proud to see the imprint of Vietnamese culture in Oklahoma. I believe our move with Jimmy's Egg helped speed up that process. It helped a conservative community embrace a refugee community, which has only enriched Oklahoma's culture. The million eggs we crack at Jimmy's Egg each year helped pave the way for Riviere Modern Banh Mi, literally and figuratively. Still, I can see where it even helped pave the way for pho, bun, and banh mi to be served from Edmond to Norman and Midwest City to Yukon.

Last year, I was humbled to be awarded as a Civic Pioneer at the Greater Oklahoma City Asian Chamber of Commerce's Silk and Spices gala. It was only the second year for the organization and the gala, which makes it all the more impressive to see. We have just finished building the ground floor to support real growth in the Asian community in Oklahoma and seeing it on display in a showcase of diverse food, dance, and decor was truly unbelievable. I stood before that crowd and told a few of the same stories you've read in this book, but they didn't know what an emotional moment it really was for me. I like to laugh and have fun, but standing there on stage before this throng of people from all over the world who had come to Oklahoma was very moving. I saw so many familiar faces. The faces of people with similar refugee stories to mine. But it was even more exhilarating to see so many unfamiliar faces. Our Vietnamese community has grown strong in its own right and has bolstered the broader Asian community into a force to be reckoned with socially, culturally, and economically. On that night, it was one big, happy family.

For us, family is like sharing a common soul. Loc and Kim founded it at Jimmy's Egg. Yen, I, and the rest of the extended family have grown it into its own kind of socio-economic force. Getting there took so much blood, sweat, and tears. It required a great deal of vision and sacrifice. I'm proud to carry the mantle today. However, I will have to step away from Jimmy's Egg one day. When that day comes, Jimmy's Egg will remain a family operation. No different than when we lost Loc and Kim so tragically. They built a strong family foundation before they left us. Jimmy's Egg has a bright future. My kids are among those who will play a role, but I raised them to stand on their own two feet first.

When Yen and I got married, we were already pregnant. That immediately put fatherhood on my mind. Like many new parents, I decided right away that I would do things completely opposite to my father's ways. Among them was to develop a closer, more intimate relationship with my kids. I see now my dad had a lot to deal with when I was growing up. He was a prominent military magistrate during a time when the entire country was at war, and he was fighting on the losing side. It's easy to see why my father didn't have much quality time to sit and talk with all eight of us kids. Yen and I wanted a family, but maybe not as big as the families we were raised in. It allowed more quality time. I spent more time hugging them, traveling, and conversing about things.

Once they entered high school, I began discussing the future with the boys. I told them we would need a CPA someday to manage the books and run the business. I told them we would need an architect to design our stores and develop the future. When Pauline came along, I always wanted her to be a lawyer. In my eyes, we needed to set the Nguyen dynasty. I also told them those are good jobs, whether you're working in the family business or not, but this was the structure I saw. James worked for Price Waterhouse for approximately five years. After seeing how complex the corporate world is, he came to me and said, "Dad, I'm ready to work for you now!"

James is now our CFO, who oversees the bookkeeping. His mom now works for him! As I mentioned in the last chapter, Pauline is a COO. I think she has a bright future expanding the Jimmy's Egg universe. If she obtains a commercial real estate license, it could mean significant opportunities in the future. Khoi and his wife Julie live in New York, where they both work as architects. During the pandemic, we had to make the hard decision to close the first Jimmy's Egg location we owned at 1616 N May Avenue. However, we own the property and plan to build a new store to memorialize Loc and Kim at the new location. Khoi has already designed the store to honor his grandparents. I expect he and Julie will act as developers on the project, and I hope that whets their appetite for more.

Meanwhile, James and his wife, Brandi, helped launch my latest obsession: grandparenthood. James and his wife were married about three years before they delivered our first grandchild, Mason Vu Nguyen. At this writing, he's barely a year old and very active. I remember when James and his wife brought the ultrasound photo to Yen and me. We all went crazy. I called the baby Peanut immediately because that's what he looked like. Like I said, Mason is a very active little guy. We expect him to be a heck of an athlete someday. Of course, I raised my kids to play tennis, just as my father raised me. We traveled all over the country for tennis tournaments growing up. James played a year at OSU, and Khoi played at the University of Oklahoma before they decided to concentrate on their studies. Little Mason may grow up and be a tennis player, too, but there's a great chance he'll play volleyball. His mom, Brandi, is an excellent athlete. She excelled in both volleyball and softball. She was so aggressive on the court, a real competitor.

Khoi and Julie went through a tragedy last year when their first pregnancy ended in miscarriage. Yen and I were heartbroken for them. I told Khoi that when a pregnancy ends this way, it means the birth wasn't meant to be. Even though his grandmother had eight kids, she also had four miscarriages. Of course, Yen and I suffered a miscarriage between Khoi and Pauline. It was a terrible, tearful loss, but I have complete confidence they will grow their family when the time is right.

That leaves little Mason to get pretty spoiled before any new cousins come along, and I am here for it. Right now, he comes over twice a week. He's not a year old yet, but he prefers Grandpa! It's been our tradition for him to hang all over me and play kissy face at family dinners. That is pretty good evidence that my grandpa game is coming along. Just as with golf, tennis, nunchucks, and business, my grandpa skills are self-taught.

With our kids starting their own families and the Jimmy's Egg family grounded and ready to expand further, you might think it's time for Yen and me to ride off into the sunset. I get it. We're getting up there. Look, I'm not blind. I have to look in the mirror every morning and see more gray hairs. I don't see any wrinkles on Yen, but I've picked up a few. I'm not saying we're ready to take that ride, but I decided long ago that we'll ride into retirement in style when the day comes. I got the idea several years ago when many of my friends started buying exotic cars. It captured my imagination, so I took rides in all of them. The one car that stood out was a McLaren. It was by far the smoothest ride I took. So, I decided to buy one. It took a year to build, but the idea of riding off into the sunset sounds more appealing. And when the day comes to ride off in style, you can best believe our first destination will be Las Vegas. We've been taking plenty of practice trips to get ready.

The End

Acknowledgments

This book would not have been possible without the love, support, and encouragement of so many people throughout my life and career.

First and foremost, I thank my incredible wife, Yen, for her unwavering love, strength, and partnership in life and business. Your grace and wisdom have been my guiding light. To my children—James, Khoi, and Pauline—thank you for inspiring me every day and for continuing the family legacy with dedication and heart.

I am deeply grateful to my parents, whose sacrifices, resilience, and values laid the foundation for everything I have accomplished. Thank you for teaching me the importance of preparation, perseverance, and faith.

To my siblings, extended family, and in-laws, thank you for your support, guidance, humor, and shared memories that made this story worth telling.

I also want to thank my mentors, friends, and colleagues who offered counsel, opportunity, and belief in me along the way.

Finally, I extend heartfelt thanks to the readers. May this story remind you that with desire, dreams, and just the right amount of dissatisfaction, anything is possible.

About the Author

Ban Nguyen's heritage is rooted in Vietnam. He is a 1.5-generation Vietnamese American who came to the US at the age of thirteen in 1975 with his family after the fall of Saigon. They resettled at a refugee relocation center in Arkansas before moving to Tulsa, Oklahoma, where Nguyen went to high school and found work as a busboy and waiter in the restaurant industry. In 2008, Nguyen's  father-in-law put him in charge of franchising the chain. As of 2025, there are over 60 locations nationwide, with more on the way. Nguyen and his family reside in Oklahoma City.

Ban Nguyen

www.ingramcontent.com/pod-product-compliance
Lightning Source LLC
Chambersburg PA
CBHW071210120626
46546CB00006B/2497